MORRIS AUTOMATED INFORMATION NETWORK

0 1029 0594040

PARSIPPANY - TROY HILLS
PUBLIC LIBRARY
PARSIPPANY BRANCH
449 HALSEY ROAD
PARSIPPANY, NJ 07054
973-897-5150

Level 5

Series editor: Nicholas Tims

The Mayor of Casterbridge

Thomas Hardy

Retold by Tim Herdon

CAMBRIDGE
UNIVERSITY PRESS

AUG 3 1 2011

CAMBRIDGE UNIVERSITY PRESS
Cambridge, New York, Melbourne, Madrid, Cape Town, Singapore,
São Paulo, Delhi, Dubai, Tokyo

Cambridge University Press
79 Anson Road, #06-04/06, Singapore 079906

www.cambridge.org

This American English edition is based on *The Mayor of Casterbridge*,
ISBN 978-8-483-23560-7 first published by Cambridge University Press in 2009.

© Cambridge University Press 2009, 2010

This publication is in copyright. Subject to statutory exception
and to the provisions of relevant collective licensing agreements,
no reproduction of any part may take place without the written
permission of Cambridge University Press.

First published 2009
American English edition 2010

Printed in Singapore by Tien Wah Press

ISBN 978-0-521-14887-0 Paperback

No character in this work is based on any person living or dead.
Any resemblance to an actual person or situation is purely accidental.

Illustrations by Lyn Knott

Audio recording by hyphen

Exercises by Peter McDonnell

The publishers are grateful to the following for permission to reproduce
photographic material:

Getty Images | Timothy Allen for cover image

Contents

People in the story

Michael Henchard: a farm worker that rises to become the
Mayor of Casterbridge; he is married to Susan Henchard

Susan Henchard: a weak woman; she is married to Michael
Henchard

Elizabeth-Jane: Susan's daughter; she has a quiet, strong
character

Donald Farfrae: a Scot that becomes very successful in
Casterbridge because of his intelligence and kindness

Lucetta Templeton: a woman that knows Michael Henchard
from the past

BEFORE YOU READ

● ●

1 Look at the cover and *People in the story*. Who do you think
the people on the cover are?

Chapter 1

Looking for work

A man and a woman carrying a little girl in her arms slowly approached the village of Weydon-Priors on foot. It was a late summer evening and the man hoped to find work in the surrounding farms. There were many villages like this in this part of southwest England, and in the early part of the nineteenth century a young man could always find work if he was prepared to look for it.

The man, Michael Henchard, was young and tall, he had a serious-looking face, and he was very sun-tanned from spending many hours working in the fields. His wife, Susan, was also young and her face might have been attractive once, but now it had the bitter look of a woman who had been badly treated by life. Although they walked side by side and they were clearly a small family, there was no sense of closeness or fondness between them. He was reading something on a sheet of paper and he seemed to almost not notice her. She, having nothing to say to him, spoke quietly and softly to her little daughter.

*   *   *

As they got closer and closer to the village, they heard the sounds of a fair. They walked toward it and came across a number of large, square tents, which were selling different kinds of food and drink. Hungry after their long walk, they decided to eat something and went into one of the tents. Inside they found people sitting at long, narrow tables that went along each side of the tent. In the middle, there was a red-faced woman serving "furmity[1]" from a big pot over a fire. This was a hot mixture of corn[2], milk, raisins, and other ingredients. The young woman ordered three bowls of furmity and they sat down to eat.

Despite being hungry, Michael Henchard did not like the mixture and wished it was a glass of beer instead. As he was thinking this, he noticed that, for a little extra money, the old woman added alcohol to the furmity of some of the others in the tent. She poured it quickly and quietly from a bottle, which she kept under the table. So he passed his bowl to her and, with a little nod and a smile, she added some alcohol to his, too. Now he found the furmity a much tastier mixture. In fact, it was so tasty that he soon asked for more.

After the first bowl he felt relaxed, and after the second he was sharing amusing stories with other men in the tent. The third made him a little aggressive, and after the fourth he was looking for trouble. The young woman saw, too late, that it was going to be difficult to change her husband's mood. Their little daughter, who had been quiet up to that point, was now tired and beginning to complain.

"Michael, it's time to leave. We have to find a place to spend the night," she reminded him, trying to pull him away from the table.

*   *   *

But Henchard was not listening to her. The conversation among the men had turned to the high ideals of youth and the low realities of later life.

"I got married when I was eighteen, like a fool," said Henchard, with bitterness. "I could have been someone important – I could have made my fortune. But instead, here I am, with only fifteen shillings[3] in my pocket and two extra mouths to feed."

It was getting late and outside the tent the fair was coming to an end. The shouts of men wanting to sell their last few animals could be heard.

"Who'll take this last horse?" shouted one man. "She's a fine animal, just a little over five years old, but there's nothing wrong with her at all. Who'll give me forty shillings for her? You won't get a better price than that."

*   *   *

Hearing these shouts from inside the tent, Henchard said in a loud voice, "Those men out there can get rid of their horses when they don't want them. Why can't we do that with our wives, too?"

One or two men laughed.

"I wouldn't be surprised if there was someone who would buy *your* wife from you. She looks like a fine woman," said one of them.

Now was a good time to stop this joke: to continue with it would not be sensible. But Henchard was in no mood to be sensible.

"Well, here's your chance. What will you offer me for this rare beauty?" he said, pointing at Susan.

"Michael, you've said things like this before, but this joke is no longer funny," said the young woman.

"I know I've said it before and I meant it. All I want is a buyer," he replied.

Raising his voice he said, "Well, is anyone interested? If you are, now's your chance."

Again there were a few laughs. Susan begged him to leave the tent, "Come on Michael, it's getting dark and I've had enough of this nonsense. If you don't come now, I will leave without you."

But Henchard did not move; it was almost as if he didn't hear her. This time his voice was even louder, "This woman is no good to me. Who among you will buy her?"

Chapter 2

The right price

Hearing this, his wife's face changed color. There was nothing begging in her voice or her expression now.

"Michael, this is getting very serious, very serious indeed," Susan said.

"Will anybody buy her?" he repeated.

"I wish someone would," Susan cried out, "for I am not at all happy with my present owner."

"There, you see? She agrees to the sale. She takes the child, I take my tools and we go our separate ways. It is as simple as that. So who'll be the auctioneer[4] for the sale?"

"I will," said a man at the same table. "Who'll make an offer for this lady?"

Suddenly the tent was strangely silent.

"Five shillings," said a voice from the back. There were a few nervous laughs.

"Only serious offers please," said Henchard. "Who'll say a guinea[5]?"

There was no answer.

"Raise the price, auctioneer," said the husband.

"Two guineas!" said the auctioneer.

"If they don't take her for two guineas in ten seconds, they'll have to give more," said Henchard.

There was silence for ten seconds.

"Very well, it's now three guineas for the lady," said the auctioneer.

"No offer? Come on, she has cost me at least fifty times that price. I tell you what – I won't accept less than five guineas for her," shouted Henchard, bringing his fist down on the table with great force as he spoke.

"If any man will pay five guineas and treat her well, he can have her forever and never hear from me again. Five guineas and she's yours. Susan, do you agree?"

His wife lowered her head in a silent yes.

"Right, you all heard that," said the auctioneer. "Five guineas, or the sale is canceled. Any offers?"

There was silence.

"For the last time, will anybody give five guineas for the lady?"

"Yes," said a loud voice from the doorway.

Everyone turned to see who had spoken. It was a sailor that had come into the tent quietly in the last few minutes. All conversations around the tent now stopped.

"Saying is one thing and paying is another," said Henchard, turning slowly to face the sailor.

The sailor took out five pounds and five shilling coins and threw them down on the table in front of Henchard. Up to this point it had all seemed like a game or a joke that had gone on too long. But now with real money on the table, the seller, the woman being sold, and the buyer were part of a drama. The air in the tent was suddenly heavy and still: everyone's eyes were locked on these three and the money that lay between them. Henchard was too surprised to react. Susan broke the silence.

"Michael, if you touch that money, Elizabeth-Jane and I will leave with this man. And you will never see us again," she told her husband slowly.

Then she added, "This is no joke, Michael."

This last comment seemed to sting Henchard into action. "Of course it's no joke," he replied. "I take the money, the sailor takes you."

"She should come with me only if she is willing. I don't mean to hurt her," said the sailor.

"She is willing, as long as she can take the child," said Henchard.

Susan looked at Michael and, seeing no change in his eyes, nodded at the sailor. She picked up Elizabeth-Jane and her few possessions and walked toward the sailor. Reaching the doorway of the tent, she took off her wedding ring and threw it at Henchard's face. Then she took the sailor's arm and left.

After this scene, there was no more to be said or done. The customers left one by one and Henchard's head sank lower and lower until it was eventually lying on the table. A few minutes later he was snoring.

*   *   *

The next morning Henchard woke up with a headache. He had some memory of the night before, but it was not clear. He had an uncomfortable feeling that he'd done something bad – *very* bad. Looking at the ground, he saw a small object – his wife Susan's wedding ring. Now he began to remember the night's unhappy events. He felt inside his shirt pocket: the five pounds and five shilling coins were proof of what had happened. He knew he had to get up immediately and find Susan and Elizabeth-Jane. Surely it would not be too late to make everything right? As he walked toward the village to start his search, he saw the church and stopped to think for a moment. Entering the church, he knelt down near the front. Looking up at the cross, he said the following words:

"I, Michael Henchard, make a promise before God – that for the next twenty-one years, the same number that I have lived so far, I will not touch any kind of strong drink."

Standing up, he had the feeling that this was the start of a new direction. He left the church to begin the search for his wife and daughter.

But it was not as easy as he thought. First of all, no one knew either the sailor or Susan; neither of them was from that area. Second, to make a big fuss about the loss of his wife and daughter would mean explaining how it had happened, and Henchard did not want all the talk and gossip this would create. So, as a result, his search was a quiet one and he made little progress. After Weydon-Priors he tried to find Susan and Elizabeth-Jane in other nearby villages, but no one had seen them and no one knew anything about them.

Henchard searched far and wide in the weeks and months that followed, but found no clue to put him on the right path. Finally he reached a port town, and here he discovered that they had sailed for Canada a short time earlier. There was nothing else to do and nowhere else to look.

Henchard now decided to go to Casterbridge, a town that he had passed through on his travels. Here, he would start a new life and try to put the mistakes of his past behind him.

Chapter 3

Looking for a relative

Eighteen years later Susan was taking another long journey on foot, but this time she was alone with Elizabeth-Jane. They were approaching the town of Casterbridge. The events that led to this second journey were as follows:

For several years she and Newson, the sailor, lived in Canada; they were not rich, but they managed. Then, when Elizabeth-Jane was twelve, they moved back to England. Here, Susan finally told a friend about the terrible circumstances of her meeting Newson. This friend told her that there was no reason to stay with Newson, that the sale of a wife was not, nor could ever be, the same as a real marriage. From that moment, Susan was certain that she had made a mistake accepting Newson as her "new" husband. But a few years later something happened to change her circumstances again: the ship that Newson was working on sank near Newfoundland. They were told that everyone had drowned; there were no survivors. Elizabeth-Jane was now a young woman of eighteen and Susan, because of her hard life, looked older than her age and was frequently sick. They were almost as poor as they had been when she met Newson, only now there was no Newson to provide an income. A month after the news of Newson's death, Susan realized that there was only one possible path toward a life of a little more comfort, a life of better opportunities for Elizabeth-Jane.

They left for Weydon-Priors on foot, following the same roads that she had taken on her journey with Michael Henchard – almost eighteen years earlier. It was the only way she knew how to try to find Henchard. In Weydon-Priors she managed to speak to the same old, red-faced woman selling furmity, who had played an important part in Henchard getting drunk. From her she learned that Henchard had come back to Weydon-Priors one year later. He had told her that if anyone should ever come looking for him, she was to say that he could be found in Casterbridge.

And so Susan and Elizabeth-Jane now started walking toward that town. Susan was exhausted from the many days of traveling on foot, but she felt sure that she would find the answer to her problems in Casterbridge. As they came closer, they could see that it was a town of a reasonable size. In fact, it was an important town in the area because of its weekly market and because it was the collection point for all the corn from the farms in the area.

"Mother, you never really explained to me what kind of relation this Mr. Henchard is to us," said Elizabeth-Jane.

It was true; Susan had kept the details of their past a secret from her daughter, although a hundred times she had come close to telling her the true story of her life.

"He is related to us by marriage," she carefully replied.

"So is he a close relative?" asked Elizabeth-Jane.

"No, not at all," Susan said quickly.

If the time came, she would tell her daughter everything she needed to know. For now it was best not to shine any more light on such a complicated and painful past.

Now they were near the center of the town, and they could hear the sound of music and loud voices coming from inside a large building that stood on one of the main streets of the town. This was the King's Arms, the main hotel in Casterbridge. Inside a large room on the ground floor of the hotel, a big dinner was in progress. It was apparently an important event because a number of people on the street were watching it through the windows.

"It might be a good idea to try and find out from one of these

people if they know anything about our relative," whispered Susan to her daughter. "You know … whether he is here, if he is well-known, what kind of position he has in the town. But it's best if you go ahead and ask – I'm too nervous," she added.

Elizabeth-Jane went and stood beside an old man that was by one of the open windows.

"What's going on tonight?" Elizabeth-Jane asked the old man.

"Well, you must certainly be a stranger," he said. "It's a big public dinner for all the most important people in the town. The gentleman at the end of the table, that's Mr. Henchard, the mayor, and then beside him on both sides are the members of the town council."

"Mr. Henchard?" Elizabeth-Jane cried out, unable to keep the tone of surprise out of her voice.

Her mother had also heard the words "Henchard, the mayor," and was gently pushing her way closer to the window to get a better look at him. How was it possible that this man had changed from the man she knew to become the mayor of an important town like Casterbridge?

Chapter 4

A bad harvest

When Susan had last seen him, her husband was young and wore the clothes of a simple man that worked in the fields. Now he was wearing fine evening clothes and the heavy gold chain of a mayor. He was still a big man but now had many gray hairs and a general thickness in the features of his face – in short, time had made many changes to the appearance and position of the man that was her husband. Elizabeth-Jane continued talking with the old man standing beside her.

"I notice that they do not serve him wine, only water."

"Oh, yes, Mr. Henchard is famous in these parts for never touching alcohol, not even a drop. They say that many years ago he made a promise in church to not let alcohol pass his lips for twenty-one years."

"Really?" asked Elizabeth-Jane. "What was the reason for such a promise?"

"Well, I don't know, but a promise made in the church is a serious thing. I think he has something like two years left. Oh, he's a strong man, there's no doubt about that. And no wife to keep him company in the evenings either – he's a widower."

"And when did he lose his wife?" Elizabeth-Jane asked.

"I never knew her. That was before he came to Casterbridge."

While they were talking, the dinner finished and the mayor stood up to make a short speech. However, Elizabeth-Jane didn't listen to it; her attention was drawn to a young man that had just joined the small crowd outside the window. He was slim, his eyes were bright, and he had a friendly, healthy-looking face: he was, in every way, very handsome. He seemed to be a stranger too, not only because of his appearance, but also because of the small suitcase he was carrying.

Meanwhile, the mayor had finished his speech and was just about to sit down again when a voice from the far end of the table asked, "A fine speech, Mayor, but what about the bad bread in this town?"

This comment seemed to touch on a matter of importance to everyone, because immediately there were others repeating the question, some of them shouting in a way that was almost aggressive.

Elizabeth-Jane turned to her neighbor again and with a raised eyebrow invited the old man to explain what was meant by this comment. He soon made it clear to her.

"Mr. Henchard's main business is wheat[6], although he owns parts of many other businesses, too. He makes his money buying and selling wheat. This year he bought a lot of bad wheat from one of the biggest farmers and then sold it on to the bakers. Everyone's angry because the bread from this wheat is terrible – it tastes awful and the bottom of the loaf is like shoe leather."

Now they heard Henchard's reply.

"You all know that the weather at harvest[7] time this year was the worst we have had in many years. Nobody could change that. But there is one change I have made – and as a result of this my business is too large for me on my own, so I've advertised for a manager to take care of the corn department. When I have him, there won't be any more problems like this."

However, this answer did not satisfy the questioner.

"But what are you going to do to repay us for the past?" he asked. "Are you going to take the bad wheat and replace it with good wheat?"

This second question stirred up more excitement. Some of the guests had drunk a lot of wine and were repeating the question in loud voices.

"If anybody can tell me how to change fully-grown bad wheat into good wheat, I'll happily take it all back," Henchard shot back, a note of anger rising in his voice. "But it can't be done." With that, he sat down again firmly.

On hearing the mayor's final words, the young man smiled, took a notebook out of his suitcase, and quickly wrote something down. Then, tearing the piece of paper out of the notebook and folding it, he approached a waiter leaning against the door of the hotel.

"Give this to the mayor at once," he said, handing him the note.

Elizabeth-Jane noticed that the good-looking young stranger had an accent she was not used to hearing, perhaps from Scotland.

"... and can you recommend a respectable hotel that's a little less expensive than this one?" he went on to ask the waiter.

"They say the Three Mariners a little farther down this road is a good place."

The Scot, which he seemed to be, walked off in the direction of the Three Mariners, and the waiter went to deliver the note to Henchard.

Elizabeth-Jane turned to her mother.

"What should we do now, Mother?"

"I have seen Mr. Henchard, which is what I wanted to do, but now I'm not sure. It is all too ..."

Elizabeth-Jane was alarmed at how shy and indecisive her mother was.

"We need to find a place to spend the night, Mother," she said, deciding that the best thing was to take charge of the situation. "Why don't we go to the same place that the young man has gone to? Perhaps it will not be too expensive."

Elizabeth-Jane's mother agreed, and so they walked off toward the Three Mariners.

The Scot's note had an interesting effect on Henchard. At first he glanced through it carelessly. But on reaching the end, he sat up and reread it more closely. The look in his eye changed.

LOOKING BACK

 1 Check your answer to *Before you read* on page 4.

ACTIVITIES

2 Complete the summary of the first four chapters with the names in the box.

> Henchard (x4)   Susan (x2)   Canada
> Casterbridge   Newson (x3)   Elizabeth-Jane
> Weydon-Priors (x2)

When ¹.............. is a young man, he makes a big mistake. One night, he drinks too much alcohol in a village named ².............. and sells his wife, ³.............. , to a sailor named ⁴.............. , for five guineas. Susan, who has had enough of his drinking, takes their daughter, ⁵.............. , and goes to live in ⁶.............. with ⁷.............. . After several years they return to England, and a few years after that ⁸.............. dies at sea. After his death, ⁹.............. is extremely poor and decides to try and find ¹⁰.............. again so that she can give her daughter a better future. She goes back to ¹¹.............. and discovers that ¹².............. now lives in ¹³.............. . He has become a successful businessman, buying and selling wheat and, as the mayor of the town, is very important. Susan hasn't seen ¹⁴.............. for about eighteen years and is surprised by the change in his circumstances.

3 Read the sentences and write T (true), F (false), or ? (the answer isn't in the text).

1 Susan doesn't know that the woman is putting alcohol into Henchard's furmity. ☐
2 Henchard starts by asking a higher price for Susan. ☐
3 Henchard has been married to Susan for three years when he sells her. ☐
4 Susan and Elizabeth-Jane walk to Casterbridge. ☐
5 An old friend tells Susan where Henchard is. ☐
6 There are only men at the dinner. ☐

4 Answer the questions.

1 Why is Susan surprised when she sees Henchard again?

2 What do the people in Casterbridge know about Henchard's past?

3 What change is Henchard going to make to his business?

LOOKING FORWARD

5 Check (✓) what you think happens in the next four chapters.

1 Henchard refuses to see Susan and Elizabeth-Jane. ☐
2 Elizabeth-Jane discovers who Henchard really is. ☐
3 The Scot helps Henchard with his problem. ☐

Chapter 5

A stranger offers help

Most of the guests had drunk large amounts of wine and the effects were now showing. Some looked as if they didn't know how they had gotten there, what they had come for, or how they were going to get back home again. Others were telling each other funny stories and their laughter could be heard all over the room. The only man not part of this general scene was Henchard himself.

"They all seem to be busy enjoying themselves," he thought. "Now might be a good time to go and find the man who wrote this note and see what he means by it."

Henchard looked around for the waiter that had brought him the note.

"Where is the man who wrote this note?" he asked him.

"Well, he's gone now, sir, but I happen to know that he's staying at the Three Mariners."

Henchard was above all a man of action, so he also set out in the direction of the Three Mariners without another thought.

*   *   *

When Susan and Elizabeth-Jane were settled in their room in the Three Mariners, Susan immediately became worried that it would be too expensive for them; they had very little money left.

"Don't worry, Mother, we will manage. I have an idea, but you stay here."

She went downstairs and found the manageress of the hotel.

"As you seem very busy tonight and my mother's a little short of money, I wonder if I could pay part of our bill by helping?"

The manageress believed in showing kindness to strangers,

and so Elizabeth-Jane started helping with the guests' suppers. The first supper she had to serve was to the room beside theirs. It was for the young man she had seen outside the King's Arms. He hardly noticed her as she came in because he was reading a local newspaper and did not look up. This gave her the opportunity to study him briefly and to notice how well his hair was cut and the fine soft hairs on the back of his neck. Having set down his supper, she left quickly and quietly before he could look up and see her. A little while later, the manageress told Elizabeth-Jane to take her own and her mother's supper up to their room. She was glad because she was very hungry indeed.

Coming into their room with the two suppers, Elizabeth-Jane saw her mother standing up with her ear beside the wall. She put her finger across her lips, meaning that her daughter should be absolutely quiet.

"It's him," Susan whispered dramatically.

"Who?" said the girl.

"The mayor."

Susan's voice shook as she spoke these words, and a daughter with a more suspicious nature than Elizabeth-Jane's might have been surprised. But she was a kind and simple girl and she suspected nothing.

"He's in the next room with somebody. Come and listen."

Elizabeth-Jane went to where her mother was standing. In fact, it was possible to hear every word of their conversation clearly because the walls were extremely thin. Mother and daughter were each interested in the conversation for different reasons and listened carefully.

"... pleased to meet you, Mr. Henchard. I am Donald Farfrae."

"And I'm very fortunate to meet *you*. You see, Mr. Farfrae, if this treatment you mention in your note works, it is just what I'm looking for. In fact, if it really does change bad wheat into good, I'll pay you well for it," said Henchard.

"I don't really want any payment for it," replied the Scot. "I'm happy to show it to you for free. I can show you right now how it works."

At this point the talking stopped. The two women heard the quiet noises of some operation concerning the wheat and then silence, as Henchard and the Scot waited to see the result. A few minutes later they heard Henchard speaking excitedly, "It's worked! The wheat is back to normal, or nearly normal!"

"Yes, it's impossible to cure it completely. But it's much better than before," replied the Scot.

"Are you sure I can't pay you for this service?"

"No, really, it's not important," insisted Farfrae.

"You're very kind, and you have saved a situation which was becoming more and more difficult." Henchard paused for a moment, as if searching for the right words.

"But listen, my business is corn and hay[8]. Hay is what I understand best, although there's much more work now with corn. If you would take … would accept the job of manager, you would have complete control of my corn department and I'd pay you a good salary. What do you say?"

Farfrae was clearly touched by Henchard's offer. "You are too kind, but no, I can't accept the position. I have a plan to go to America and my heart is set on it. I want to see the world."

"Are you sure, Mr. Farfrae? It is a great pity, truly a great pity. I'm not very good with the science part of things, or with the numbers. You're the opposite – I can see that. I have been looking for a man like you for two years now, but it seems it is not to be."

"I'm truly sorry," replied Farfrae, "but I think that I will regret it if I don't make this great trip."

It was late and Farfrae had to be up early the next day to take the coach[9] to Bristol, where he was sailing for America. They said their good-byes, and Elizabeth-Jane and her mother quietly moved away from the wall and prepared to go to bed. As Elizabeth-Jane was falling asleep, she found herself thinking of Farfrae. She wondered if it was possible that something might happen to make him stay in Casterbridge instead of going to America.

Chapter 6

A change of plan

The next morning was one of those mornings in late summer when the coming of fall is in the air. Henchard was walking down the middle of the street, going over the conversation with Farfrae in his mind. He was no longer wearing the fine clothes from last night, but was dressed for business instead. Passing the Three Mariners, he noticed that the man he had met the previous evening was standing at the window of his room on the first floor.

"So you are off soon, I suppose?" asked Henchard, looking up.

"Yes, any moment now, sir," replied Farfrae. "In fact, I was thinking of walking a little of the way and letting the coach catch up with me."

"Well, why don't I walk with you to the top of the road?"

"All right, but give me a minute," said Farfrae.

A few minutes later Farfrae came out of the hotel, carrying his bag. They set out together.

"Ah, young man, I still think you should stay here and work for me."

"Well, perhaps I should. To tell you the truth, my plans are not very clear – I just know that I want to see the world."

*   *   *

They continued walking together, not speaking much. They came to the highest part of the town. From here they could see the beautiful forests and fields of England stretching out in every direction. From this road there was a narrow path leading down to the main road between Bristol and Bath below them. Farfrae would have to go down this path to meet his coach.

"Well, I wish you success," said Henchard, holding out his right hand for Farfrae to shake. "I shall not forget this time and how you helped me in a moment of great difficulty," he continued.

Still holding the young man's hand firmly in his own, Henchard decided to try one last time to make Farfrae change his mind.

"I'm not the kind of man who lets an opportunity go without a fight. I want to ask you again – will you stay and work for me? If you will, just tell me the salary you want and I'll gladly pay it. I'll be open with you – I like you Farfrae, you're a good man!"

Farfrae said nothing for a moment. He looked out over the beautiful countryside beneath them and then back at Henchard.

"This is not what I planned. But perhaps it is fate[10] … life is telling me what to do. Should you go against your fate? No! I won't go to America – I'll stay here and take that job!"

"Done," said Henchard.

"Done," said Farfrae and they shook hands again. Then they walked back into the town to have a large breakfast at Henchard's house and talk about the details of the job and the salary. Both men felt very pleased with the way things had developed that morning.

*   *   *

Beside the room that Farfrae had left only an hour ago, Elizabeth-Jane and Susan were sharing a simple breakfast. Elizabeth-Jane examined her mother's face.

"What are you thinking about, Mother?" asked the daughter.

"I am thinking that Mr. Henchard seemed to behave very kindly toward that young man and he only met him last night," answered her mother. "Surely if he behaves so warmly with people he doesn't know, then he will be even kinder to his own relatives?"

Elizabeth-Jane agreed, but it was not that simple: her mother then found several reasons not to ask this important relative for

help. However, Susan then remembered two things: that he still lived alone, and that he felt sorry for his great mistake in the past. At last she made up her mind.

"You have to take a message to him from me. You will tell him that his relative Susan, a sailor's widow, is in town. It will be his decision whether he agrees to see me. If he would prefer not to because of his position as mayor of the town, we will understand. We will leave quietly, without a fuss, and go back to where we came from."

"And if he wants see us?" asked Elizabeth-Jane.

"Then ask him to write me a note, saying when and how he will see me. But make sure you tell him that we do not come here expecting anything at all."

*   *   *

Elizabeth-Jane set out to find Henchard. It was market day in Casterbridge, and she enjoyed the sights and sounds of the busy market as she walked slowly down the main street. People came from all over the surrounding countryside to buy and to sell. There were many different kinds of food for sale: great piles of fruit and vegetables on tables that had been set up outside the stores. In other parts of the street there were animals for sale: pigs, chickens, and horses. Indeed, the street was so crowded with all the people, animals, and food that it was difficult to get from one end to the other.

She arrived at Henchard's house but could not find him at first. She went around to the back of the house where a number of men were at work, but there was no sign of Henchard there either. Eventually, a young boy showed her an office she hadn't seen before; she knocked on the door.

"Come in," said a voice.

She went in and was very surprised to see, not Henchard, but Donald Farfrae.

31

"I'm sorry, is … is Mr. Henchard here?" she asked.

"He's busy, but he'll be free in a minute, if you can just wait a little?" replied Farfrae, and he found a chair for her to sit on near his desk.

Having done this, he immediately returned to the work that Henchard had hired him to do just an hour or so earlier.

A few minutes later the door to Henchard's inner office opened, but just as she was about to stand up and talk to Henchard himself, a man came in and, walking straight into Henchard's inner office, introduced himself, "Joshua Jopp, sir. I'm the new manager that you hired."

"The new manager! He's in his office," replied Henchard, without bothering to explain that the job had just been given to another man.

"In his office?" said Jopp amazed.

"I asked you to come on Thursday and as you didn't come, I have given the job to another man."

"Sir, you said Thursday or Saturday," replied Jopp, taking a letter out of his coat pocket.

"Well, you are too late," said Henchard. "There's no more to be said."

"But you more or less said that the job was mine," objected Jopp.

"Depending on your interview," replied Henchard. "I am sorry for you, very sorry indeed. But it can't be helped."

There was nothing more to be said and Jopp turned to go. Elizabeth-Jane could see that he was shaking with anger. As she entered the room, Henchard turned around to look at her.

"Now, what is it that you want, young lady?"

"Can I speak to you about a personal matter, sir?" she asked.

"Yes, of course," answered Henchard, looking at her with sudden curiosity in his eyes.

"I have been sent to tell you, sir, that a relative of yours, Susan

Newson, a sailor's widow, is in the town. She would like to know if you wish to see her."

Henchard's face, normally dark from spending many hours outside, went slightly pale.

"Susan … she is … still alive?"

He spoke quietly and seemed to trip over these words.

"Yes sir. She is alive."

Chapter 7

Repayment

It took Henchard a few seconds to take in the news that Susan was still alive. But he controlled his feelings carefully. If Elizabeth-Jane knew nothing of the past, it was important not to give her any reason to suspect anything.

"Are you her daughter?"

"Yes sir, her only daughter – Elizabeth-Jane."

"Elizabeth-Jane Newson?"

"Yes, Elizabeth-Jane Newson."

So the girl didn't know their strange family history. That was good.

"So, your mother is well?"

"She is rather exhausted with traveling."

"Her husband was a sailor ... yes, I understand – when did he die?"

"Father was lost at sea last spring."

Henchard found it hard to hear the word "Father" used by Elizabeth-Jane in this way. He asked a few more questions and then made a decision. He sat down at the table and wrote a few lines. Taking five sovereign[11] coins from his wallet, he put these and the letter inside an envelope, which he sealed[12] carefully.

"Elizabeth-Jane, I would like you to take this letter to your mother. Deliver it to her personally please. I am very glad to see you here, Elizabeth-Jane. We need to have a long talk together, but not just now."

Saying good-bye, he held her hand so warmly that she, having known little warmth or friendship in her life, was touched by his kindness.

Elizabeth-Jane took the letter and the money straight to her mother. Susan was moved by the sight of a letter from her husband, but she did not open it at once. After asking Elizabeth-Jane a few questions about their meeting, she eventually opened the letter and read it:

Meet me at eight o'clock this evening at the Ring – it's easy to find. I can say no more now. The girl seems to know nothing – keep it like that until I have seen you.
M. Henchard

Susan folded the note and told Elizabeth-Jane that she was going to see Henchard that evening.

*   *   *

The Ring was an old Roman ruin just outside the town. It was a lonely place and certainly not a romantic place for lovers of any kind to meet. Henchard had chosen it because it was easy to find for someone new to Casterbridge. Also, because he was mayor of the town, he could not invite Susan to come to his house until they had a definite plan of some kind. He arrived just before eight o'clock and saw that she was already there. Neither spoke at first – there was no need – and poor Susan leaned against Henchard, who supported her in his arms.

"I don't drink now, Susan. I haven't since that night."

Those were his first words.

"I looked for you everywhere. There was every reason to suppose that you and Elizabeth-Jane had died. Tell me, why did you keep silent?"

"For him of course!" replied Susan, almost crying. "I thought I had to be faithful to him. He had paid so much for me. If he hadn't died, I would never have come."

"How could you be so foolish? Now listen, we have to think

of a plan. I suppose you've heard that in this town I'm the mayor and an important businessman and so on?"

"Yes," she said quietly.

"These things, as well as keeping the truth from Elizabeth-Jane, mean that we have to be extremely careful. So I don't see how you two can come and live in my house as the wife and daughter I once treated badly."

"We'll go away at once," said Susan timidly.

"No, no, you misunderstand me," replied Henchard. "Here's

my plan – you and Elizabeth-Jane take a cottage as the widow Mrs. Newson and her daughter. I have a certain cottage in mind already. I meet you, visit you, and marry you. You come and live with me, with Elizabeth-Jane as my step-daughter."

"I am in your hands, Michael. I came here for Elizabeth-Jane – for my part, if you told me to leave tomorrow, I would."

"Now, now, don't speak like that. Think about my plan. If you can't think of a better one, that's what we'll do. Are you all right for money at the moment? Let me know when you need more."

"We are fine at the moment, perfectly fine. I think I like the idea of us marrying again. But now I have to get back to Elizabeth-Jane and tell her that our relative wishes us to stay in Casterbridge. Don't follow me. It's too risky – someone might see us together."

"Right," said Henchard. "But just one more thing. Do you forgive me, Susan?"

She mumbled an answer but was unable to say a clear yes or no.

"Never mind. Judge me by how I act in the future," said Henchard firmly.

Susan set out again in the direction of the Three Mariners. Her heart was beating wildly after so much change in such a short time. Nevertheless, she could not help feeling that being with Henchard again could bring her and Elizabeth-Jane a number of new problems. She hoped she would be strong enough to face them.

Chapter 8

Two women and one man

When Henchard got home, he saw a light shining in the office window. Farfrae was still at work, sorting out all the records, bills, and papers connected with Henchard's business. He went in to see him.

"Still there? It's late. Come – you should do no more work tonight. There's always tomorrow. Come and have some supper with me. I insist."

Farfrae had little choice but to agree because Henchard reached over and closed the books forcefully.

They enjoyed a simple supper and afterward they sat together by the fire. Its cheerful warmth seemed to encourage the friendship that was growing between these two men.

"It's strange that we have met each other purely through business and yet, at the end of the first day, I find I wish to speak to you about a personal matter," Henchard told Farfrae. "But I'm a lonely man and I have no one else to talk to."

"I'm glad to help if I can," said Farfrae politely, although he was tired after a very busy day. He couldn't help thinking that some rest might be preferable to a long talk with Henchard.

"I've not always been what I am now," continued Henchard. "Can you believe that I was a married man once?"

"I heard in the town that you were a widower," replied Farfrae.

"A widower, yes, that's what they think. But the truth is that I lost my wife nineteen years ago, through my own fault … this is how it happened. One summer evening we were traveling from village to village on foot – me, my wife, and our baby. I was looking for work. We came to a furmity tent in a country fair. At that time I was a drinking man."

As Henchard told all the details of how he sold his wife and daughter and how he searched for them everywhere afterward, Farfrae became more and more interested and no longer thought about rest. Henchard went on to tell him about his promise not to drink, made nineteen years ago, and how he had buried his loneliness in work, rising to become the man he was today.

"… and in all that time I heard nothing from my wife, nothing until today. For today she has come back!" said Henchard, enjoying the drama of this part of his story.

"She has come back?" cried Farfrae, in shock.

"Yes, she has, this morning."

Henchard told him how he had received the news from Elizabeth-Jane and how he had met Susan earlier that evening. He also told him that both he and Susan agreed that, for now, Elizabeth-Jane should not know the truth.

"But what's to be done now?" asked Henchard.

"Can't you just take her back and live with her? Make up for[13] the past?"

"That's what I thought, too. But Farfrae, by doing right with Susan, I do wrong to another woman," Henchard said sadly.

"How do you mean?"

"For many years I have made business trips to Jersey, especially during the potato season. One year I was ill[14] when I was there. A very elegant and intelligent young lady was staying in the same hotel as me. She took pity on me and decided to take care of me till I was better. Little by little she fell in love with me, although I don't know why – I'm not worth it. One thing led to another and we became lovers. Of course Jersey is a small island and people have a way of finding things out. There was a scandal[15] and I came back to Casterbridge. The scandal didn't affect me, but it ruined her good name. In letter after letter she told me how she was suffering, until I realized that I had to do something. I told her that if she was prepared to run the risk of Susan being alive, we should get married. She was very happy when I suggested this and we probably would have married soon. But now … Susan appears!"

These last few words were said with a bitter laugh. He went on, "How did I get into such a mess? I suppose it's impossible that a man like me could go through twenty years without making more than one great mistake. As things are, I will disappoint one of these women – and it has to be the second one. My first duty is to Susan – that's clear to me. But I wish I could show the second woman some kindness. I do not want to hurt her."

"Ah well, there's nothing to be done," said Farfrae. "You just have to write to the young lady and explain why she cannot be your wife and wish her well."

"No, I have to do more than that for her. I will write to her and send a reasonable amount of money. She always talked about some rich uncle or aunt, but I'm sure that the money will be very useful to her anyway. But I'm not good with words – would you help me write her a letter, explaining what's happened as gently as you can?"

"Of course, I'd be glad to help you," replied the good Scot.

He took the paper and pen that Henchard handed him and a little while later the letter was written. As Farfrae was leaving, Henchard said, "It's a great comfort to me to tell all of this to a friend. You see now that the Mayor of Casterbridge's family life is not as healthy as his pocket!"

"I do indeed," replied Farfrae, "and I feel sorry for you!"

The next morning Henchard copied the letter in his own handwriting, put it inside an envelope with a check, and took it to the post office.

"Is this going to work?" he thought, as he was mailing it. "Who knows? And will I be able to make up for the past with Susan?"

LOOKING BACK

 Check your answer to *Looking forward* on page 23.

ACTIVITIES

2 Match the two parts of the sentences.

1 Although Henchard offers Farfrae money for his help, ☐
2 Farfrae doesn't accept Henchard's job offer at first ☐
3 Henchard hires Farfrae ☐
4 Henchard wants to meet Susan, ☐
5 Henchard met the woman in Jersey when ☐
6 Henchard isn't going to marry the woman in Jersey ☐

a he was on a business trip.
b although he has already offered the job to someone else.
c because he wants to make up for the past with Susan.
d he doesn't accept it.
e because he has other plans.
f but he doesn't want people to see them together.

3 Put the sentences about Henchard's relationship with the woman in Jersey in order.

1 Henchard and the woman become lovers. ☐
2 The woman falls in love with Henchard. ☐
3 Henchard's wife returns. ☐
4 Henchard and the woman decide to get married. ☐
5 The woman looks after Henchard. ☐
6 People say bad things about the woman. ☐

4 Read the sentences from the text and answer the questions.

1 The only man not part of this general scene was Henchard himself. (page 24) Why is Henchard not part of the scene?

....

2 Susan says, "We will leave quietly, without a fuss ..." (page 31) What can you tell about Susan's character from this?

....

3 Susan says about Newson, "I thought I had to be faithful to him." (page 35) Why does Susan feel like this?

....

4 Henchard doubted that he "could go through twenty years without making more than one great mistake." (pages 40–1) What are the two "great mistakes" he has made?

....

 5 Answer the questions.

1 What was in the note Farfrae sent to Henchard?

....

2 What advice does Farfrae offer Henchard about the woman in Jersey?

....

LOOKING FORWARD

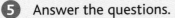

 6 What do you think happens in the next four chapters? Answer the questions.

1 What happens to change Henchard and Farfrae's friendship?

....

2 What happens with the woman from Jersey?

....

Chapter 9

The dance

The next few months were good times of change and growth for everybody. During work hours Henchard and Farfrae were almost always together. They could be seen walking down the street, with Henchard's big arm thrown over the narrow shoulders of his manager. He seemed to value the Scot's company just as much as he valued his judgment in business matters. And, at the end of the day, Henchard would often insist that Farfrae come over to his house for some supper. It was as if he was making up for all the years of loneliness by throwing all his energy into this friendship.

Farfrae's presence was also very good for business. Where previously deals[16] had always been agreed by word, Farfrae introduced a method for properly recording everything that was bought and sold. Where previously business had always progressed in stops and starts, through misunderstandings, mistakes, and delays, now it ran as smoothly as a train on rails. People soon began to make comparisons between Farfrae's and Henchard's way of doing things. Everything that Farfrae was involved in seemed to go well and he quickly earned the respect of Casterbridge society at all levels. From the man in the field that saw how well he understood wheat, weather, and water, right up to members of the town council that saw what a good head for business he had – everyone liked his confident, kind way of dealing with people. As if this was not already a very full range of talents, he was also very good-looking, he sang beautifully, and he danced with a true understanding of the poetry of movement. He was therefore very attractive to women, who found him impossible to resist.

Henchard was not deaf to the town gossip about Farfrae, and some of the comparisons that he heard people make did annoy him. However, for now his mind was more occupied with other matters. He was following the plan he had explained to Susan when they met at the Ring. One afternoon, when she and Elizabeth-Jane were settled in their little cottage, he visited them. He stayed for tea and was invited to come back another day. Elizabeth-Jane suspected nothing of a secret past and Henchard seemed to enjoy the visits. He visited with increasing frequency, to the point where Casterbridge society started to comment on a possible marriage between the widow Newson and their mayor. One afternoon when Henchard visited, Elizabeth-Jane was out.

"This is a good opportunity for me to ask you to name the happy day, Susan," he said.

"Oh, Michael, I'm afraid that this has caused you a lot of trouble – I didn't expect so much," replied Susan.

"Oh, nonsense, it's no trouble at all."

No man could have been more energetic than Henchard in the preparations for the wedding. He personally made sure all the arrangements were right. But the truth was that Henchard took no great pleasure in his second wedding to Susan, neither in the days leading up to it, nor in the ceremony itself. His thoughts were entirely focused on making up for the past, and on bringing his daughter and his wife to live under his roof. He also knew that Casterbridge society considered Susan Newson to be a very small fish for the mayor and, as a result, their general opinion of him had gone down. But he felt that he deserved[17] this as a kind of punishment and accepted it.

* * *

Perhaps the person for whom the changes were greatest was Elizabeth-Jane. In the past she had known little comfort and, except for her clothes, she had had very few things to call her own. Now she lived in a large, beautiful house with servants and could ask for anything that caught her eye. She dressed with good taste and found that people began to notice her more. As the fall, winter, and spring passed, her thin face and figure filled out with rounder and softer curves, and her skin began to have a healthy color. Confidence in herself and the absence of worry added to her growing beauty.

On top of this, she was happy. Henchard was very fond of her and they both took great pleasure in walking together; in fact, she now went out with Henchard more frequently than with her mother. Another reason for her happiness was that she had fallen in love, although perhaps she herself wasn't sure what name to give this feeling. Farfrae was the man who stirred these feelings in her and she did what she could to try and see him, although this was never easy.

One evening there was a public dance organized by Farfrae to celebrate the start of spring. Elizabeth-Jane was excited about it all day: this was a good opportunity to see a little more of Farfrae. She went in her best dress, accompanied by Henchard and her mother.

When they arrived, a string band was playing a lively Scottish dance and Farfrae was in the middle of the crowd, spinning wildly and throwing himself in all directions in time to the music. Henchard noticed that Elizabeth-Jane could not take her eyes off Farfrae. He felt his blood beginning to rise, but turned away to talk to a friendly man that he knew from the town council. When he looked at Farfrae again, the Scot was doing a more elegant dance – with Elizabeth-Jane. She was not as good a dancer as he was, but she was enjoying herself greatly. When it ended, she smiled at Henchard but, instead of smiling back at her, he looked away angrily.

"Farfrae's done a splendid job here, don't you think?" said his friend from the town council. "And doesn't he dance well? You'd better watch out," he continued in a joking way, "he may find more ways of showing he's the better man."

46

"No, he won't be doing that," said Henchard, his blood now boiling.

The dance had ended and Farfrae was now near enough to hear him.

"He won't be doing that because he'll soon be leaving me."

He looked straight at Farfrae. "Mr. Farfrae's time as my manager is coming to an end, isn't it, Mr. Farfrae?"

Farfrae quietly said yes and walked away.

It was getting late and Elizabeth-Jane decided it was time to go home. As she was leaving, she heard Farfrae calling her.

"Wait, Miss Newson, I've been looking for you everywhere. Would you mind if I walked with you to the corner of your street? It seems that I'm going to leave you soon."

"Why?" she said, her voice shaking a little.

"Well, no special reason … actually I think I hurt your father's feelings by organizing this event …" Farfrae replied, adding, "it's a pity because I hoped to have one more dance with you."

"But I dance so badly."

"No, you don't," Farfrae said warmly. "It's the feeling for it rather than knowing the exact steps – that's what matters."

He paused for a while before going on. "I wish I was richer, Miss Newson, and I wish I had not made your father angry. I would like to ask you something … but now it can't be."

What he would have asked her, he didn't say, and she was not experienced enough to encourage him to say it. So they walked the rest of the way in silence, afraid of the unspoken words between them.

Chapter 10

An important letter

The next morning, when Henchard's jealous mood had passed, his heart sank at what he had done and said. He felt even worse when he learned that Farfrae had taken his words seriously.

Farfrae stopped working for Henchard, but he didn't leave Casterbridge. A man in the corn and hay business, whose business was much smaller than Henchard's, wanted to sell and Farfrae bought it from him. However, it was not his intention to be in competition with Henchard. He considered that the Casterbridge market for corn and hay was easily big enough for both of them and that they needn't worry about stealing each other's customers. Henchard, however, immediately saw it as a personal attack.

"Didn't I help him when he came here with his pockets almost empty?" he shouted at the next meeting of the town council.

"Didn't I give him a job and tell him to name his own salary? Well, if he wants a fight, I'll show him! I'll buy and sell till there's nothing for him, till his business comes crashing down! He'll be sorry for this!"

When Elizabeth-Jane heard of Farfrae's decision to stay in Casterbridge, it made her heart beat faster, but now Henchard put an end to her romantic dreams.

"Elizabeth-Jane, I've seen you talking with Farfrae two or three times. Have you promised him anything?" he asked her.

"No, I haven't promised him anything," she replied.

"Good, because I do not want you to see him again."

"Very well, sir."

"Do you promise?" he asked her, looking at her straight in the eyes.

"Yes sir, if you wish it," she replied, her heart sinking.

"I *do* wish it. He is an enemy to this house."

Henchard immediately wrote a note to Farfrae, asking him not to visit or speak to his daughter again. Another man in his shoes would have encouraged Farfrae to become his son-in-law. This would have been an elegant solution to the risks of future competition in business, but such a way of thinking was completely foreign to Henchard. He either loved a man or hated him, and his wife was not strong enough to persuade him to see things differently.

* * *

Around this time Susan, who had never had good health, got very sick. Henchard immediately sent for the best doctor money could buy. For a while she seemed to improve, but it was only temporary.

One day, when she seemed especially weak, she asked for a pen and paper. After writing for a while, she carefully folded and sealed the paper with wax. On the front it said, "To Mr. Michael

50

Henchard. Not to be opened until Elizabeth-Jane's wedding day." She locked it in her drawer.

After this her condition worsened steadily. Elizabeth-Jane sat with her night after night and tried to make her as comfortable as possible, but it was clear that her life was slowly draining away. One night she told her daughter that she would have liked her to marry Farfrae. After that she no longer spoke, and by morning she was dead.

The next few weeks were a time of great sadness for Elizabeth-Jane, although the death of Susan did bring her closer to Henchard. In the evenings they often sat looking at the fire, sharing a comfortable silence.

"Was Newson a kind father to you?" Henchard asked his daughter one evening.

"Yes sir, very."

"Suppose I had been your real father?" he said. "Would you have cared as much for me as you cared for him?"

"I don't know. I couldn't say. I can only think of *him* as my father."

Henchard had first lost Farfrae and then Susan in different ways; now it seemed that the only hope left for him was Elizabeth-Jane. He said nothing at first, torn between the desire to tell the truth or to continue as before. Eventually he couldn't stand it any longer. He told her that he and Susan had been married many years ago and had then been separated. He did not give the details of how this had happened and, of course, did not mention how or why he had sold her mother. He ended by explaining that Newson was not her real father. Elizabeth-Jane sat quietly listening to Henchard's explanations, her face white, but after a while she became very upset and burst into tears.

"Don't cry, please don't cry," he begged her. "I can't bear it – I am your father. Why should you cry?"

Elizabeth-Jane tried to answer, but her voice was shaking so much she couldn't speak.

"Don't blame me for what happened in the past," he went on. "I was a drinking man before and I was unkind to your mother. But I'll do anything if you'll look on me as your father. I won't say any more now. I'll leave you to think about it till the morning, or you decide when. And I'll show you some papers that prove what I have been saying."

Having said this, he left the room and went upstairs to find those papers. Opening the drawer of the little table by his bed, he saw Susan's papers, which he had kept there since her death. There was a letter addressed to him that he hadn't seen before: "Not to be opened until Elizabeth-Jane's wedding day."

However, the wax of the seal had broken a little and the letter was in fact open. Henchard had no reason to think he was doing anything wrong by opening a letter that was probably not of very great importance. He read the following:

My dear Michael,
For the good of all three of us I have kept one secret from
you till now. I shall be in my grave and Elizabeth-Jane will
have a home. Please try to understand why I did not tell
you before what I am telling you now: Elizabeth-Jane is not
your daughter. That child died three months after you sold
me. This living one is my daughter with Newson. I gave her
the same name to fill up the emptiness left by the death of
the first. Tell Elizabeth-Jane's husband this, or not, as you
prefer. And please forgive me just as I forgave you for what
you did.

Susan Henchard

Henchard looked up from the letter. He felt as if he had grown twenty years older. All of the satisfaction he felt just a little while ago, when he told Elizabeth-Jane that she was his daughter, was now a bitter taste in his mouth. He sat without moving, thinking with a heavy heart of the order in which recent events had happened. If he hadn't told Elizabeth-Jane her past history, he wouldn't have needed to find those papers. If he hadn't searched in his drawer, he wouldn't have found Susan's letter. It was a cruel blow: he had asked Elizabeth-Jane to call him Father and immediately after discovered that she was, in fact, no relative of his at all.

It was a night of little sleep, and Henchard came down to breakfast in the morning with dark thoughts in his mind. He was not prepared for Elizabeth-Jane's reaction.

"Good morning Father," she said warmly, taking his arm.

"I've thought about what you told me all night and I see you are my real father. Now I understand why you've treated me so kindly since I arrived in Casterbridge. A stepfather wouldn't have been so good to me. Mr. Newson was very kind, but that's not the same as being my real father. So, Father, breakfast is ready," she finished, smiling at him cheerfully.

Without thinking, Henchard leaned over her and kissed her on the cheek, but he was in a state of shock. For weeks he had waited for the moment when she would accept him as her father. Now that it had finally come, he saw that the palace of his dreams had crumbled to dust.

Chapter 11

A new friend

Elizabeth-Jane found it impossible to understand the sudden change in her father's attitude. The evening he had told her his past history, he had been full of love and concern, but the next morning he was cold and distant in a way she had never seen before. He started having many of his meals away from home, seeming to avoid her company as much as possible. On the few occasions when he did speak to her, it was in a tone of bitter criticism. One day he got angry because she used words that a farm worker would use, not a young lady. Another time he criticized the way she wrote, asking where she had learned such uneducated handwriting.

For his part, Henchard now started to feel that it was a mistake to have told Farfrae to stay away from Elizabeth-Jane. He wrote him a note:

> *Sir, having thought about the matter again, I am no longer against your seeing Elizabeth-Jane, if you care for her. All I ask is that you do not see her in my house.*
>
> *M. Henchard*

Elizabeth-Jane was sad and confused at the new attitude of Henchard and started going for long walks by herself. One spot she visited every morning on these walks was her mother's grave. On a day when she felt especially sad, she was sitting on a bench nearby, looking at the place where her mother lay buried.

"Oh, I wish I was dead with dear Mother!" she said louder than she meant to.

Suddenly she noticed someone standing just behind her; she turned to look. It was a young lady, beautifully dressed, very pretty, and with lively, kind eyes. Elizabeth-Jane's face went red.

"Yes, I heard you," said the lady in a friendly way. "What can have happened?"

"I don't – I can't tell you."

Elizabeth-Jane felt embarrassed, and yet there was something about the stranger that comforted her.

"Then I will guess – that was your mother," said the lady, waving toward Susan's grave.

"Yes, that was my mother, my only friend."

"But your father … is he alive?"

"Yes, he is alive," replied Elizabeth-Jane.

"Is he not kind to you?"

"I can't complain of him," replied Elizabeth-Jane.

"But perhaps you've had some kind of argument, is that right?"

"Yes, perhaps." Elizabeth-Jane didn't know why this elegantly dressed young lady wanted to know about her, but she sensed that she could trust her.

"I think he is angry with me because I'm not very educated. And my poor education is because of my past."

"What is your past?" asked the young lady.

"I'm afraid my past is not very interesting. But I can tell it to you, if you really want to hear it."

"I really want to hear it," replied the young lady.

And so Elizabeth-Jane told her her life story, as she understood it. She ended with Henchard's unkind and cold treatment of her.

"I am thinking of leaving home. But what can I do? Where can I go?"

"Well, perhaps I can help," offered the young lady. "I shall soon need someone to live with me, partly to take care of the house and partly to keep me company. But perhaps you …"

"Yes, please, yes!" Elizabeth-Jane cried. "I would do anything to be independent, for then my father might grow to love me. However …"

"However what?" asked the young lady.

"Well, you see I'm not very educated and you would need someone educated."

"No, not necessarily," replied the young lady.

"Really? But there's something else. I never learned good handwriting and surely you would need someone with good handwriting?"

"Well, no, not really."

Having arranged for Elizabeth-Jane to move into the young lady's house the following week, they said good-bye at the church gate.

* * *

One or two days later Henchard noticed that a number of men were moving some luggage into a large town house that had been empty for some time. He wondered what kind of person would be moving into such a grand house. His curiosity was satisfied when he received a letter in handwriting he knew well:

My dear Mr. Henchard,
Don't be surprised – I have moved to Casterbridge. I heard
of the death of your wife – poor woman; hers was not an
easy life. I decided to come here and ask you to carry out
the promise you made to me some time ago. I hope you still
think the same as you did when we last spoke about this
matter. Not knowing your situation, however, I decided to
come here first and find out for myself. The aunt I told you
about in Jersey died recently and left me enough money, to
allow me to live in some comfort. I am renting High Place
Hall. I shall be able to see you in a day or two.
Lucetta

Henchard was surprised by the letter. What was the meaning of Lucetta suddenly coming to live in Casterbridge like this?

He liked to be the one in charge, and he was worried by the independent spirit Lucetta showed in her letter.

Elizabeth-Jane was worried that Henchard would be against the idea of her moving out. She decided to wait until she found him in a good mood. But she needn't have waited – Henchard no longer seemed to care at all what she said or did. She told him that she had been offered a position, which would allow her to improve herself. He didn't ask her who she was going to work for, or where or for how long. However, he agreed with her that he would pay her an annual amount of money, which would give her some independence. Elizabeth-Jane thought sadly that he seemed to be offering her this money more out of a desire to get her off his hands than out of any interest in her as a daughter.

Elizabeth-Jane saw the elegant young lady again at the same place in her walk, a few days later.

"Your father is willing to let you go?"

"Yes, he is," replied Elizabeth-Jane.

"Then come."

"When?" asked Elizabeth-Jane.

"Today, now – as soon as you like."

To be out of her father's house that very day – the idea was an attractive one. Henchard was not at home when she returned. She decided to organize the move immediately and ordered her things to be put in a carriage[18]. While this was happening, Henchard returned from work.

"Are you leaving already?" he said to her through the window of the carriage.

"You said I could, Father," she reminded him.

"Yes, but I didn't think you would be going so quickly. Is this how you treat me after all I've done for you?"

"Father, how can you speak like that? It is completely unfair," she said, her voice rising with feeling.

Up until then Elizabeth-Jane had accepted his criticism, without question, believing herself to be truly at fault. Henchard saw for the first time how his cold, distant attitude had hurt her.

"Look here, Elizabeth-Jane, maybe I have not been as kind to you recently as I should have. But it's because of something important to do with you."

"To do with me? What is it?" asked Elizabeth-Jane.

"I can't tell you just now. But if you'll just continue living here as my daughter, I'll tell you one day."

But Henchard's attempt to make peace had come ten minutes too late.

"Father, I think it's best for both of us that I leave now. But I shall not be far away and, if you really need me, I can come back."

"Not far away?" asked Henchard. "What will the address be, in case I need to write to you?"

"It's right here in the town," said Elizabeth-Jane. "It's High Place Hall."

She waved to him and then signaled the driver to start. The carriage moved slowly out into the street. Once again, it seemed to Henchard that life was playing a cruel trick on him.

Chapter 12

Old love and new love

Henchard was frustrated[19]. But this mood didn't last long, as he soon received another letter from Lucetta:

You will know by now of my arrangement with your daughter. Please don't think that I am playing some kind of game with you, and believe me when I say that we met by accident. She feels she has been treated unfairly by you. But the most important thing is that you now have a good reason to visit me. You can call on me as if you were visiting her and Casterbridge society will not find it strange.

Lucetta

Henchard was delighted with the letter and admired Lucetta's intelligent thinking. Sitting alone at his dining room table, he considered the meaning behind these words. She certainly seemed to be interested in marriage and was clearly encouraging him to take the first step. Forgetting his frustrated feelings about Elizabeth-Jane, he realized that he wanted to see Lucetta very much. Since he never put off anything he wanted to do, he immediately set out for High Place Hall. But on arrival he was told by the servant that Lucetta was busy that evening and would be pleased to see him the following day. In fact, Henchard had come at a moment when Lucetta and Elizabeth-Jane were deep in conversation about their personal lives. Henchard, however, did not know this and was not pleased.

"Women! Why are they never straight with you?"

He decided that it was now his turn to keep *her* waiting and therefore he would not visit her the next day.

The next morning Lucetta dressed carefully, in a way she knew Henchard would find attractive. She waited for him all morning, but he didn't show up. The afternoon came and went, but still he didn't come. Almost a whole week went by this way. Each day she dressed with the same care, and each day came to an end without a visit from Henchard. However, she was not bitterly disappointed. In the early days she had been deeply in love with him, but after all the difficult times she had gone through, her feelings were no longer as warm. Her wish to be married to Henchard had more to do with making up for the past than any great love she might still feel for him.

The morning of market day came. Lucetta knew that Henchard would be doing business with various farmers almost directly under her window.

"Perhaps your father will call on you today?" she said to Elizabeth-Jane.

"No, he won't come," said Elizabeth-Jane shaking her head sadly.

"Why not?"

"His heart is set against me," said Elizabeth-Jane in a shaky voice.

"So your differences are bigger than I thought."

"Yes, they are," said Elizabeth-Jane, close to tears.

"So where you are is the place he is most likely to avoid?"

Elizabeth-Jane nodded. Shocked, Lucetta realized that her plan had gone completely wrong. The only way to see Henchard would be to get Elizabeth-Jane out of the house for the rest of the morning. She therefore thought up a number of small jobs for Elizabeth-Jane to do around the town and, when she was alone, wrote a quick note to Henchard:

I am sadly disappointed that you have not come to call on me yet. Your daughter's presence may be the reason for this, so I have sent her out for the whole morning. Say that you come on business; I shall be alone.

Lucetta

She told her servant that if a gentleman called, he was to be shown in immediately. She then sat down to wait. She did not have long to wait – she heard the door open and then the footsteps of a man on the stairs outside. In a moment of sudden shyness, she hid herself behind the curtains. The visitor was shown into the room and the servant shut the door behind him. Lucetta dramatically threw back the curtain. The man in front of her was not Henchard.

Her visitor was younger than Henchard, fairer and more handsome.

"Oh, I'm sorry, I thought …" Lucetta began. She was embarrassed but also a little amused.

"Perhaps I made a mistake. I asked for Miss Henchard and the servant showed me in. My name is Farfrae, Donald Farfrae. Perhaps I have come to the wrong house?" said Farfrae, looking worried.

"Oh no, now that you are here, please do sit down," said Lucetta quickly. "I am Lucetta Templeton, Miss Lucetta Templeton." She said the word "Miss" carefully. "Miss Henchard will be here soon."

There was a short silence: after such an unusual beginning, Lucetta and Farfrae were not sure how to continue the conversation.

"The market today is a big one, isn't it? It's interesting to look out of the window and see everything going on," said Lucetta.

"Do you look out often?" asked Farfrae.

"Yes, very often," replied Lucetta.

"And do you look for anyone you know?"

"Well, not really … but now I may look for you!"

Lucetta was surprised at her own openness and quickly added a safer explanation for her words.

"What I mean is that it's comforting to see a face that you know in the crowd."

"Perhaps you are a little lonely here?" asked Farfrae.

"Nobody knows how lonely."

"But they say that you are rich."

"If so, perhaps I don't know how to enjoy my riches," answered Lucetta.

They continued talking for a long time, easily changing from one subject to another. Farfrae was very different from the kind of person Lucetta normally met, and she found him extremely interesting. His moods seemed to change quickly, but in a way she found charming: one moment he was talking excitedly about business in Casterbridge, the next he was talking sadly about how much he missed the mountains and lakes of his homeland. At some point, Farfrae realized that he had important business to do with people at the market, and yet he seemed unable to leave the company of this attractive woman. Eventually, he forced himself to get up.

"I'll come another time, if I may," he said.

"Certainly," replied Lucetta. "What has happened today is very curious."

"Perhaps something to think about when we are alone."

"Yes, perhaps it is," she replied. "But whatever it was, it's now over and the market calls you."

"Yes, yes. Business! I wish there was no business calling me!" said Farfrae with feeling.

Lucetta almost laughed.

"How you change when you talk!" she said.

"But it's only since coming here and seeing you."

"Well, if seeing me has this effect on you, perhaps seeing me is not a good idea."

"But whether I see you or not, I'll see you in my thoughts," said Farfrae looking straight into her eyes, and then he left to return to his business duties. He had completely forgotten that the original reason for his visit was to see Elizabeth-Jane.

A few minutes after he left, there was a loud knock on the front door. Lucetta's servant came into the room.

"The mayor," she said, "and he doesn't have much time, he says."

"Oh well, in that case tell him that, as I have a headache, it would be better if he called another day instead."

LOOKING BACK

 Check your answers to *Looking forward* on page 43.

ACTIVITIES

2 Read the sentences and write T (true), F (false), or ? (the answer isn't in the text).

1 At first Henchard is pleased with the changes Farfrae makes in the way his business is run. ☐

2 Farfrae is happier working in his own business than working for Henchard. ☐

3 Susan never forgave Henchard for selling her to Newson. ☐

4 Henchard wishes he hadn't told Elizabeth-Jane that he was her father. ☐

5 Elizabeth-Jane thinks that Lucetta is very intelligent. ☐

6 Henchard is angry with Elizabeth-Jane because she doesn't behave like an educated woman. ☐

7 Elizabeth-Jane wishes Henchard loved her. ☐

8 Lucetta pretends to be sick in order not to see Henchard. ☐

3 Underline the correct words in each sentence.

1 People in Casterbridge had a *lower / higher* opinion of Henchard after he married Susan.

2 *Henchard / Newson* is Elizabeth-Jane's father.

3 Lucetta says that she *knew / didn't know* who Elizabeth-Jane was when she first met her.

4 Henchard goes to High Place Hall to visit *Lucetta / Elizabeth-Jane*.

5 Farfrae goes to High Place Hall to visit *Lucetta / Elizabeth-Jane*.

6 Lucetta falls in love with *Michael / Donald*.

4 Read the sentences from the text and answer the questions.

1 People soon began to make comparisons between Farfrae's and Henchard's way of doing things. (page 44)
Who do people prefer – Farfrae or Henchard?

....

2 ... it made her heart beat faster ... (page 49)
How does Elizabeth-Jane feel here and why?

....

3 "I decided to come here and ask you to carry out the promise you made to me some time ago." (page 57)
What was the promise Henchard made to Lucetta?

....

4 She said the word "Miss" carefully. (page 62)
What is Lucetta telling Farfrae here?

....
....

5 Answer the questions.

1 How does Henchard feel about his second wedding to Susan?

....

2 Why does the friendship between Henchard and Farfrae end?

....

3 Why does Lucetta come to Casterbridge?

....

LOOKING FORWARD

● ●

6 Check (✓) what you think happens in the next four chapters.

1 Henchard and Lucetta get married. ☐
2 Henchard becomes very poor. ☐
3 Farfrae leaves Casterbridge. ☐

Chapter 13

Two men and one woman

Elizabeth-Jane noticed the change in Lucetta immediately and sensed that Lucetta had met a man who had had a strong effect on her heart. There were many clues to help her: the extra care Lucetta took with her clothes, the way she looked out of the window as if trying to see someone in particular, and her general manner, which was more excitable than before. After observing her friend for some time, the name of the man that had such an effect on Lucetta was clear.

One day at breakfast Lucetta was very nervous. She had slept very little, and there was clearly something important that was worrying her. She told Elizabeth-Jane that she was very worried about a friend of hers and needed to ask Elizabeth-Jane's advice. Elizabeth-Jane, being naturally kind and understanding, sat down to listen.

"This friend was once very fond of a man. They were very close in a … physical sense," said Lucetta.

It was difficult to say these things in a direct way, but she hoped that Elizabeth-Jane understood what she meant.

"She was fonder of him than he was of her. But to make the situation acceptable, he asked her to marry him. She agreed. But then there was an unexpected problem and the marriage never took place. Nevertheless, she felt she could now not belong to another man. They were separated by distance and by circumstance and, not hearing anything from him for a long time, she felt her life offered her no opportunities."

"Oh, poor woman," said Elizabeth-Jane with feeling.

"Yes, it was hard and she suffered greatly because of him, although I should say he was not to blame for everything that happened. Anyway, a long time later the reason for their separation disappeared, and he came to her to offer marriage again."

"How wonderful!" said Elizabeth-Jane.

"But meanwhile, she had seen another man and this man she liked more than the first. Could she say no to the first man, because of the second man?"

"Oh, that would be bad," said Elizabeth-Jane.

Lucetta looked hurt and said, "Yes, but then again you have to remember that she was forced into an unacceptable position with the first man. It was not one she chose. And that he was not as well-educated as the second."

"I cannot answer," said Elizabeth-Jane thoughtfully. "It's a very complicated situation."

"Cannot, or perhaps will not?" asked Lucetta.

"Will not," said Elizabeth-Jane truthfully.

But Lucetta was not hurt by Elizabeth-Jane's answer. She was clearly happier, having told Elizabeth-Jane what was worrying her, and seemed much less nervous than before. They said nothing more about the subject. Later that night in bed, Elizabeth-Jane wondered why Lucetta had not trusted her enough to tell her any of the names in the story, because it had been clear from the beginning who the "she" of Lucetta's story was.

Who the second man in the story was became even clearer on the day that Farfrae came by to have tea. It looked like he was visiting Elizabeth-Jane, and at first it did, in fact, seem as if he was talking to her as well as to Lucetta. But it soon became obvious that he only had eyes for Lucetta. When Elizabeth-Jane spoke, he answered in single words, but when Lucetta said something, he hung on her every word. Elizabeth-Jane left the room as soon as it was possible to do so without appearing rude.

Meanwhile, Henchard was discovering that his strategy of ignoring Lucetta was not successful. His feelings toward her had changed a great deal in the last week. She was no longer a woman he felt sorry for, or a woman he felt he owed a debt[20] to. Her more mature beauty, together with the difficulty of managing to see her, had made her, in his mind, the woman he desired more than anything else in life. He decided to visit her again.

However, when he was there standing in front of her, it did not go as he had imagined.

"It is so good of you to call on me," she said with a cool politeness that he found confusing. In her beautifully decorated living room, seeing her in her most elegant clothes, he felt like a farm worker.

"Well, of course, I have called on you," he said. "And you know the reason why I have called. I have come to say that I am ready to give you my name in return for your becoming my wife. You can fix the date and the month, for as soon as you think is acceptable – you know more of these things than I do."

"Well, it is a little too soon," she replied.

"Well, perhaps, but it is an honest offer and it will make those who criticized you in Jersey keep quiet."

"How can you say that?" she cried out.

It made her angry that he thought he was doing her a favor.

"My only crime was allowing myself to act on the strong feelings I had for you. I suffered enough for that mistake in the past, and then it was even worse when you wrote to tell me of your wife's return. If I have a little independence now because of my aunt's money, I think I deserve it."

Henchard had not expected this reaction from Lucetta.

"Ah, I see," he said. "So what do you say to my offer?"

"I say you should treat me just as someone that you know and I will do the same. Time will …" she said, not sure how to finish the sentence.

"So that's how it is, then?" said Henchard, looking down at his feet like a defeated man. At that very moment, Farfrae rode by the window on horseback. If Henchard had looked up then, he would have seen the reason for Lucetta's less than warm attitude, because her face lit up. But he missed this clue to her behavior, and he could see no way of improving things between them, so he left.

There was now a period of time when both Farfrae and Henchard frequently visited Lucetta. Elizabeth-Jane felt as if she hardly existed in this world; she was ignored by the man she believed to be her father, and ignored by the man that had once wanted to win her heart. The pain of rejection that she felt was made a little easier to live with by a kind of bitter humor in the contrast between the way they treated her and the way they treated Lucetta. When Lucetta cut her finger, they were as worried about it as if she was dying, but when she herself was really sick, both men simply said something polite to her and then forgot all about it.

Elizabeth-Jane could not help wondering what she had done to make Henchard ignore her so completely. On the other hand, she could understand Farfrae's changed attitude toward her. After all, in the night sky she was a small star compared to the beautiful moon of Lucetta's beauty. She had gotten used to life taking away what she wanted and giving her what she didn't want. So it was with patience that she waited to find out what unwanted event life would send her to replace the loss of Farfrae's love.

Chapter 14

An agreement to marry

Henchard still did not have definite proof that Lucetta was in love with Farfrae, but he knew it would not be long before he had it. Meanwhile, the suspicion of this was enough for him to want to hurt Farfrae in any way possible. An idea began to form in his mind. He sent for Jopp, the man that he had treated so unfairly when he gave Farfrae the job of manager.

"Once again I need a manager. Are you available?" he asked Jopp.

"Yes sir, I am," replied Jopp.

"In that case, the job is yours. When can you start?"

"As soon as you wish, sir."

"Good," said Henchard, and then he leaned forward and looked deep into Jopp's eyes.

"Now listen. The Scot who is getting so much of the town's hay and corn business – he has to be cut out. Do you understand me?"

"Perfectly," replied Jopp.

"But fairly and honestly. We'll buy hard and sell hard until he can't take it anymore. I have the money and I can do it."

"I'm with you all the way," said Jopp. Ever since the day that his job had been given to Farfrae, he had had his own reasons for hating the Scot. This made him the right partner for revenge, but a very unsuitable partner in business. They stayed in Henchard's office till late at night, planning the details of how to squeeze Farfrae out of business.

The most important time of the year for Casterbridge farmers and businessmen was approaching: the wheat harvest. The size and quality of the harvest depended completely on the weather. Too much rain at the wrong time could make a big difference to the harvest, and this in turn would affect the price of wheat. Men like Henchard and Farfrae had the job of judging the right moment to buy and the right moment to sell. Taking a clever risk at the right time could make a man wealthy – getting it wrong could break him. All of this depended on the weather: at this time of year Casterbridge people seemed to be constantly talking and thinking about the weather.

Henchard had a strong feeling that the last two weeks of August would be very wet. So he waited until the middle of August and then bought up all the wheat he could. Day after day he bought wheat and only stopped when there was absolutely no room left to keep it. Pleased with his work, he waited for the weather to turn bad. But the last two weeks of August were fine, finer than usual. The sun shone brightly every day and the skies were a brilliant blue. Everyone talked about an excellent harvest, and the price of wheat fell like a stone. Henchard now had a very large amount of wheat that was worth much less than what he had paid for it. He was forced to sell it; his losses were terrible. Just when he finished selling everything, the bad weather arrived and the price of wheat went up again. If he had waited just a few more days to sell, he wouldn't have made a profit[21], but at least he would have avoided such heavy losses. But Henchard always acted fast before thinking, and without a good manager to advise him and make him slow down, he was lost. Farfrae, on the other hand, waited until the right moment to buy and to sell, and made a large profit.

*   *   *

Soon after this Henchard had to go to the bank. He spent the whole morning there watching everything that belonged to him, everything that he had built up over the years, be taken by the bank. Coming out of the building, he met Jopp. Still angry from his discussions inside the bank, he pushed Jopp against the wall.

"If it hadn't been for your advice, none of this would have happened," he shouted at the unfortunate Jopp. "Why did you let me go on, when a word from you would have made me think twice?"

"My advice, sir, was to do what you thought best," said the other.

"What a useful manager! And the sooner you're useful to someone else in that way, the better. Find yourself another job!"

Henchard said no more and walked off down the street. The color drained from Jopp's face.

"You'll be sorry for this, sir. Sorry as a man can be!"

* * *

The effect of these events was to make Henchard even more desperate. In trying to ruin Farfrae, he had, in fact, ruined himself. But matters then got even worse: one day walking to the fields he accidentally heard a conversation between Farfrae and Lucetta. They spoke of love and marriage.

"Why should Farfrae have the satisfaction of ruining my hopes for marriage as well as my business?" Henchard said to himself angrily.

He came up with a plan. He walked quickly back to Casterbridge and straight to Lucetta's house. He knew she would be alone, because Farfrae had other business later that day. He arrived before her and went straight into her living room. He didn't have long to wait. When she walked in, she didn't see him at first and let out a small scream.

"You frightened me! And what are you doing here? It's ten o'clock, and you have no right to surprise me like this in my own home."

"I don't know whether I have no right – but I certainly have an excuse. There is a little matter that I need to remind you of."

"No, I don't want to hear it," said Lucetta, sinking into a chair.

"But you ought to hear it," said Henchard, coming close to her.

"It all came to nothing and because of you, not me," she replied. "If you wanted to marry me for love, then I might feel that I had a duty toward you. But my feelings for you changed when I realized that you only felt sorry for me."

"Admit it, you became fond of another man. Although he's no better than I am," said Henchard.

"If you were as good a man as he, you would leave me alone," she shouted.

Unfortunately, this comparison with Farfrae had the effect of making Henchard even angrier.

"You cannot refuse me. Unless you promise tonight, in front of a witness, to become my wife, I will tell everyone what happened between us in the past. It is only fair that other men should know this."

There was now a look of bitter sadness on Lucetta's face. If she had loved any man other than Farfrae, Henchard might have felt sorry for her. But this was not possible, and Elizabeth-Jane was sent for. She was surprised to find Henchard in the house.

"Elizabeth-Jane, I want you to hear this," he said to her, taking her hand. Turning to Lucetta: "Will you, or will you not marry me?"

"If that is what you want, I have ... no choice!"

"So you say yes?"

"I do."

No sooner had she said this than she fainted. Elizabeth-Jane rushed to help her.

"Father, why do you make her agree to marry you? You shouldn't force her into this – her health isn't strong and she can't take much."

"Don't be simple. This will leave *him* free for you."

"Leave who free?" asked Lucetta, beginning to sit up again.

"No one, as far as I am concerned," said Elizabeth-Jane firmly.

"So it is agreed?" said Henchard.

"Yes, it is agreed," said Lucetta, seeming only half alive. "But Michael, don't make me talk about it anymore."

Henchard picked up his hat and left the house.

"What is this?" asked Elizabeth-Jane, kneeling beside Lucetta. "You called my father Michael as if you knew him well. What power does he have over you? I can't understand how he can force you to do this. I'll go and speak to him and ask him to release you."

"No, don't, it's no use. Let it be," said Lucetta, her face suddenly looking old and tired.

Chapter 15

The return of the old woman

While he was having breakfast the next morning, Henchard thought about what had happened in Lucetta's house. Yes, he had acted quickly and now Lucetta was his. Farfrae would learn that not everything can be stolen.

Feeling satisfied with himself, he walked to the courtroom[22]. One of his duties was to hear and judge various cases of troublemaking. Today there was only one case – it concerned a very old woman that had been drinking and causing trouble near the church at night. After hearing the details of the case, Henchard asked the old woman if she had anything to say.

"Yes," she replied, suddenly smiling. "Nearly twenty-one years ago I was selling furmity in a tent at the fair at Weydon-Priors."

Henchard looked up at her.

"A man and a woman with a little child came in and they had a bowl each. In those days I used to add a little rum[23] to those who paid extra for it. The man had so much of it he got drunk and started arguing with his wife. He offered to sell her to the man who would pay most for her – a sailor came in, paid five guineas for her, and took her away with him. And the man who sold his wife that night is sitting there in that big chair," she finished, pointing dramatically in Henchard's direction.

Everyone looked at Henchard, whose face had now gone a strange gray color. There was a short silence, which was broken by Henchard's assistant.

"We don't want to hear ridiculous stories. You've been asked if you have anything to say which concerns your case," he said.

"It's not ridiculous. It proves that he is no better than I and has no right to sit there in judgment over me!"

"Be quiet now, that's enough of your silly stories!" said the assistant.

"No, what she says is true." The words came from Henchard.

"And it does prove that I am no better than her, so I will not be the one to judge her," he said, rising from the judge's chair and leaving the courtroom.

*   *   *

News of what had happened in the courtroom spread around Casterbridge like wild fire. Soon everyone knew that almost twenty-one years ago Henchard had sold his wife and child to a sailor at a fair.

From this moment there was a definite change in his fortune. It was the end of Henchard as an honest, respected man, and the beginning of Henchard as a desperate man. People that he owed money to all wanted to be paid immediately. Perhaps they reasoned that if a man was prepared to sell his family, he would have little conscience[24] about money that he owed. As a result, Henchard's ruin was now complete. He was forced to sell his house and his furniture, and search for the cheapest possible rooms to rent. The only place he could afford was in a small, damp house in the worst part of town, near the river. Jopp was the owner of the house and lived there, too. He took bitter satisfaction in the power he now had over Henchard, the man that had treated him so badly not once, but twice.

Now Lucetta thought about her promise to Henchard with horror. How could she go ahead and marry a man like this? She was also very afraid that if Farfrae heard about her promise, or about her past relationship with Henchard, she would lose her one opportunity for love and happiness.

She therefore decided that they had to act immediately. She went away for three days to Bredon, telling Elizabeth-Jane that she needed a change of scenery. Farfrae secretly met her there and they got married. On returning to Casterbridge, Farfrae had his things moved from his house into High Place Hall. This, of course, created a very difficult situation for Elizabeth-Jane. Lucetta, not suspecting any kind of previous interest between Elizabeth-Jane and Farfrae, invited her to stay with them in the house. She had grown very fond of Elizabeth-Jane and didn't see why she should move out if she was comfortable there. But to Elizabeth-Jane the idea of living in the same house as the man who had almost loved her was impossible. So she did move out, to a much smaller house across from the big house where Henchard used to live.

When Henchard found out that Lucetta had married Farfrae despite her promise to him, he was furious. Just when he thought something was finally his, there was Farfrae again, stealing it from under his nose. But he still had one important weapon left – the letters that Lucetta had written to him years ago from Jersey. These letters talked of their past relationship, and Henchard knew that, used at the right time, these letters would cause a lot of damage.

Chapter 16

Changing houses

One afternoon Henchard was standing on a bridge near the house he now shared with Jopp, staring into the river and thinking about how his luck had recently changed.

"She and Farfrae are moving into their new house today," said Jopp, who had come up behind him.

"Oh," said Henchard, not really listening. "Which house is that?"

"Your old one."

"Moving into my house? Of all the houses in the town, it has to be my old house?"

"Well, look at it like this – someone has to live there and as it can't be you, it might as well be him."

Farfrae had already bought the stores when Henchard had been forced to sell everything, and it had made sense to buy the house as well.

"And it seems that he was the one who bought all your furniture as well," continued Jopp, enjoying this opportunity to hurt Henchard. "They didn't even have to move it out of the house for the sale."

"My furniture, too! What will he want next? My heart, my body?"

"Perhaps … why not? If you're willing to sell them."

And he walked off, leaving Henchard to continue staring sadly into the river.

*   *   *

A little while after that Farfrae himself appeared, on his way back home from business in that part of Casterbridge. He held out his hand to Henchard.

"Henchard, it is you, I thought so," he said. "They say that you are thinking of leaving Casterbridge – is it true?"

Henchard was quiet for a few minutes before replying, "Yes sir, I am. It's strange, isn't it? A few years ago, you were thinking of going to America and I made you change your mind. On that day we stood together like this, you without a penny to your name, while I was the owner of the house in Corn Street. Now it's the other way around."

"Yes, it is the way of the world," replied Farfrae. They started walking together. "But I asked you for a good reason. Don't go. Stay at home."

"But I have no choice. The little money I have left won't last long and I will have to find work. The best chance I have is somewhere new."

"No, but just listen for a moment," said Farfrae. "I mean come and live with us in your old house. We can easily spare some rooms, we have more than enough. I'm sure my wife wouldn't mind, until you find some work."

"No, no," said Henchard. "It wouldn't work, we would argue. But I thank you for your offer anyway."

"Well look, we are not far from the house – will you come and have a little supper with us?" said Farfrae.

"No, no – it is very kind of you."

"A pity. Ah yes, I meant to say another thing. I bought a great deal of your furniture."

"So I heard."

"It's not that I really need it. But I'd like you to choose those pieces that you want to keep for yourself and take them to your house. We don't need that much and we can always get some more."

"But what do you mean, take it from you for nothing?" asked Henchard, surprised.

"Well it's probably worth much more to you than it is to me," said Farfrae.

"No, I couldn't possibly but … sometimes … I sometimes think … that I judged you wrongly," said Henchard, tripping over his words.

He was embarrassed and, saying good-bye, he started walking back to Jopp's house.

* * *

Not long after this, Elizabeth-Jane heard that Henchard had a bad cold. She went to visit him, but as she opened the door he said, "Go away, go away. I don't want to see you."

But Elizabeth-Jane decided not to listen to him. No one believed in him anymore, and he needed someone to care for him and give him back his confidence.

Over the next few days, she looked after him and he got better. Things seemed to improve a little for Henchard, and he discovered a new fondness for Elizabeth-Jane. He no longer thought about leaving Casterbridge to find work. When he was well enough to get up, he decided it was time to swallow his pride and he went to Farfrae to ask for work. Farfrae agreed to help him, but he decided that it would be best if they didn't deal with each other directly. So Henchard was hired through one of Farfrae's assistants.

For a while this worked. Henchard had gone back to the kind of physical work that he had done when he first arrived in Casterbridge twenty-one years ago, but he didn't complain. What renewed his hatred toward Farfrae was that Farfrae might become the next mayor of Casterbridge. Henchard had the feeling that Farfrae, little by little, had pushed him to the ground and was now walking all over him. Around this time, people noticed that Henchard had started talking to himself, sometimes angrily in a low voice, sometimes laughing out loud:

"Ha, a man as young as him, going to be mayor. But then I'll bet that his wife's money helps. Here I am, working under him and now he's the boss, everything I had is now his … my house, my furniture, and the woman who should have been my wife … all his now!"

And sometimes others heard him say things like, "Only two weeks to go! … only twelve days to go!"

The men who worked with him asked him what he meant by this.

"Only twelve more days before I am released from my solemn promise not to touch strong drink," replied Henchard. "In twelve days it'll be exactly twenty-one years, and then I plan to enjoy myself."

LOOKING BACK

 1 Check your answer to *Looking forward* on page 67.

ACTIVITIES

2 Complete the sentences with the names in the box.

Lucetta	Farfrae	Henchard (x3)	Elizabeth-Jane

1 .... asks someone to marry him.

2 .... loses a lot of money.

3 .... makes a lot of money.

4 .... threatens to give away a secret.

5 .... makes a promise but doesn't keep it.

6 .... takes care of someone who's sick.

3 Read the sentences and write T (true), F (false), or ? (the answer isn't in the text).

1 Henchard asks Lucetta to marry him because he feels sorry for her. ☐

2 Farfrae is happy when Henchard buys up all the wheat he can. ☐

3 Jopp hates Henchard even more than he hates Farfrae. ☐

4 After what happens in the courtroom, people in Casterbridge don't trust Henchard. ☐

5 Lucetta marries Farfrae quickly to make Henchard jealous. ☐

6 Farfrae buys Henchard's furniture because he likes it. ☐

7 Elizabeth-Jane goes to take care of Henchard even though he tells her not to. ☐

4 What do the <u>underlined</u> words refer to in these lines from the text?

1 "I suffered enough for <u>that mistake</u> in the past..." (page 70)

....

2 "If it hadn't been for your advice, none of <u>this</u> would have happened ..." (page 75) ....

3 "Yes, <u>it</u> is agreed ..." (page 77) ....

4 "No, <u>what she says</u> is true." (page 80) ....

5 <u>This</u>, of course, created a very difficult situation for Elizabeth-Jane. (page 81) ....

 5 Answer the questions.

1 How does the weather ruin Henchard's plan to hurt Farfrae?

....

2 How does Henchard's life change in these four chapters?

....

3 How does Henchard plan to use the letters he received from Lucetta?

....

4 What change is there in Henchard's feelings toward Farfrae at the end of Chapter 16?

....

LOOKING FORWARD

• •

 6 Check (✓) what you think happens in the final chapters.

1 Elizabeth-Jane discovers that Henchard isn't her father. ☐
2 Lucetta leaves Farfrae for Henchard. ☐
3 Farfrae dies. ☐

Chapter 17

Twenty-one years

He was true to his word. On the day that the twenty-one years finished, he celebrated by getting very drunk in the Three Mariners. And from that day on, he was a regular customer there in the evenings. When he had had too much to drink, which was frequently, he would tell anyone patient enough to listen to him about his unjust treatment and about how he would teach Farfrae a lesson one day.

It was only a question of time before Farfrae heard about these threats.

"Why does he hate me so?" Farfrae asked his wife one evening, after supper.

"I could understand that he might not like the fact that I've done well in business whereas he has done badly, but this fierce hatred of his … I don't understand it."

"Why don't we do what I suggested before, dear Donald?" replied Lucetta. "We have enough money. We could sell the business and move to another town."

"I know we did talk about that. But the councilors[25] are going to put forward my name for mayor, and if that's what they want, I won't say no to them."

From that evening on, Lucetta was extremely nervous. Henchard was clearly jealous, and who knew how far a jealous man was prepared to go? She decided that she had to get her old letters back as soon as possible. She met Henchard by accident a day or two later in the market. It was a busy market day and no one would hear them talking.

"Michael, I have to ask you to return any letters or papers you have of mine," she said to him. "You can see how important it is for all of us that the evidence of what happened in Jersey is destroyed."

"I will look for them," Henchard replied, enjoying Lucetta's obvious nervousness.

They went their separate ways. When Henchard was alone again, he realized that the letters were, in fact, in the safe that used to belong to him, which was still in his old house. So, at noon the next day, he went to see Farfrae and they agreed that Henchard should come for the letters that evening.

Henchard arrived at the house after first going to the Three Mariners for a few drinks. It was a strange feeling to be going back to his house for the first time, to ring the bell and to hear it from outside the house, not inside. The letters were indeed in the safe and Farfrae handed them to Henchard. Instead of taking them and leaving, Henchard began looking through them.

"Ah yes, interesting to see these letters again," he said, a little smile playing on his lips.

"Do you remember that strange chapter in my past that I told you about and that you gave me advice on? These letters are connected with that time. Although now, thank God, it is all over."

"What became of the poor woman?" asked Farfrae. He would have preferred not to have this conversation and to be upstairs with Lucetta. But Farfrae was a kind, naturally polite man and he settled down to listen.

"Luckily she married and she married well. But at the time, she was very angry. Just listen to how she used to speak." And he read part of one of the letters out loud, in which Lucetta complained bitterly of the way Jersey society treated her.

"That's how she always talked to me, when what happened was a problem that I had no way of solving."

"Yes, that's how it is with women," replied Farfrae. In fact, he had very little knowledge of women, but what Henchard read to him reminded him strongly of the way that Lucetta talked. He supposed that in matters of love all women talked in the same kind of language.

Henchard took another letter and read parts of that one out loud, too. Meanwhile Lucetta, who had been resting, heard Henchard's voice and came to the top of the stairs. She listened to the whole conversation between her husband and Henchard with increasing horror. Did he intend to tell Farfrae that she had

written those letters? If so, her marriage would be ruined. Her heart started beating very fast.

"I won't say the name – that wouldn't be fair," Henchard was saying. "When I came forward to do as I had promised, she was not the woman for me."

"Because she married this other man?"

"Yes," replied Henchard.

"She must have a heart that moves easily from one to another!" said Farfrae.

"Yes, she does."

Henchard read a couple more of the letters, but each time stopped short of reading the name. His plan had been to tell Farfrae the name of the writer as a grand finish to the evening, but in the end this was too cruel, even for Henchard.

By this time Lucetta was close to having a nervous breakdown. At last, the men's conversation ended and they went to the door.

"If I were you, I'd destroy those letters," said Farfrae. "If they ever came to light, they would greatly damage this woman and her husband."

"No, I shall keep them for the moment," said Henchard and he left.

Lucetta ran back to her bedroom and threw herself on the bed, her whole body now shaking and tears running down her face.

The next day she wrote Henchard a letter:

I heard your conversation with my husband yesterday evening, and I see that you are taking revenge on me. Have pity on a woman who is in pain. If you could see me, you would not continue in this cruel way. I beg you once again to return those letters to me.

Lucetta

And indeed, Lucetta's appearance had changed completely. Her nerves had never been good, and the worries of the last few days had made her face look tired and pale.

When Henchard received the note that evening at Jopp's house, he immediately felt sorry for what he had done. Had he sunk so low that he found enjoyment in attacking a woman, a woman he had once loved? He decided he would stop using the letters against Lucetta and Farfrae and give them back to Lucetta, as she had asked. He took them out of his drawer and went downstairs. Jopp was sitting in front of the fire.

"I wonder if you could do me a small favor, Jopp," he said. "Could you take this package to Mrs. Farfrae's house, tonight if possible? I would go myself, only I don't want to be seen there."

"Yes, I'll take it there if you like," said Jopp, reaching for the package.

"Thank you," replied Henchard, "that's kind of you."

Henchard went straight up to his bedroom. Jopp was curious about the contents of the package – why would Henchard send something to Farfrae's wife? And why not return it to her in person? It was easy to push a knife under the wax and gently open the package. As he suspected, the package contained letters. Having satisfied his curiosity, he set out for Farfrae's house, wondering how he could use the information he held in his hands.

Chapter 18

The skimmity-ride

On the way to Farfrae's house, Jopp passed a pub named Peter's Finger. This was a very different place from the Three Mariners. It was a place for people who had troubles, for people who were in trouble with the law, for people who caused trouble of different kinds. In short, trouble and the pub Peter's Finger always went together. Just outside the pub, two friends recognized him and invited him to come in for a drink.

After one or two drinks, Jopp was in the mood for some fun. He opened the package of letters and spread them out on the table.

"Look what we have here friends," he said. "These letters, believe it or not, are all from Mrs. Farfrae to Mr. Henchard."

He picked up a letter and read some of it out loud. He did the same with a few others. It soon became clear to everyone around the table what kind of relationship there had been between the two.

"Well, heavens above, Mrs. Farfrae wrote that … so she's not as respectable as she seems," said one woman. "And just think, now she's married to Farfrae, not Henchard."

She thought for a while. "You know what's needed here? A skimmity-ride[26]."

This suggestion caused a lot of laughter and shouting around the table.

"The last one seen in Casterbridge must have been at least ten years ago."

There was then a great deal of talk about how the skimmity-ride should be organized, when they should do it, and so on. This discussion was interrupted by the voice of a stranger.

"What do you mean by a skimmity-ride?" he asked. Everyone

looked around to see who had asked this question. It was a tall man with a kind, sun-tanned face.

"Well, if I remember rightly, it's a way of telling the whole town that a man and a woman have done wrong together, if you get my meaning. It's meant to embarrass them. You make a couple of models of them, using clothes and something for their faces and hair, and then you tie these models to a donkey. Then we all walk around the town with the models sitting on the donkey and we make a great big noise with pots and pans and musical instruments, so that everyone sees what's going on."

"Aha, I see," said the stranger. "I'll look forward to seeing that. And when do you think this will happen?"

"Just as soon as we can organize it. Maybe in the next few days," replied the other.

"Then I shall see it. I'm going to be in Casterbridge for a couple of weeks."

He soon got up to go and he was followed a little later by Jopp, who took the letters to Lucetta's house, as originally planned. The rest of the company continued to laugh and drink at the table while they made plans for the skimmity-ride.

*   *   *

A few days later Lucetta was in her living room, quietly waiting for the return of her husband, who had business out of town that day. It was about eight in the evening and, looking into the fire, she was thinking about how things seemed to have improved a little in the last few days. Henchard had returned the letters as promised and she had carefully burned every single one in the fire. Henchard himself had not made any kind of trouble since the evening he talked to her husband. Perhaps now she would be able to enjoy the happiness that married life with Farfrae promised, and which she so richly deserved.

At that moment, she heard a strange noise coming from

outside. She went to the window and opened it. Leaning out she could hear the noise steadily coming closer, but it was still some distance away. It sounded like a music band of some kind, but the sound itself was not at all musical. And there seemed to be a lot of people shouting and laughing as well. The noise came closer.

In her house, not far from there, Elizabeth-Jane also heard the noise. She put her hat on and went outside to see what was going on. As soon as she saw all the people and the reason for the noise, she knew she had to reach Lucetta's house as quickly as possible. She was there in two minutes and rushed straight up the stairs and into Lucetta's living room. The noise was now in the same street as the house they were in.

"Lucetta, please come away from the window, you don't need to see that nonsense," shouted Elizabeth-Jane.

She ran to Lucetta and tried to gently pull her away from the window.

"No, I want to see it," replied Lucetta, pushing her friend away firmly.

Now it was directly below them. A large group of people were making noise with anything they could find in their houses: pots and pans, violins, flutes, drums, sticks. They were shouting and laughing, and many of them were looking up at Lucetta. In the middle of this group there was a donkey, and sitting on the donkey there were two figures. One of them was a man. With the mustache and beard he was clearly meant to be Henchard. The other model was wearing a fine dress and carrying a small green umbrella.

"It's me, isn't it?" Lucetta screamed. "Look, she even has my green umbrella. Donald's on his way home now. He'll see this, won't he? He'll see it and then he won't love me anymore." Her whole body was shaking as she cried, "This will kill me, it'll kill me."

Elizabeth-Jane didn't know what to do. At that moment Lucetta fell to the ground, her body still shaking. Elizabeth-Jane

told the servant to call the doctor. He arrived soon after and examined Lucetta.

"She's had a nervous breakdown," he said to Elizabeth-Jane, who had decided not to leave her friend's side. "It's very serious. Where is her husband?"

"He's had to go out of town. He'll be back soon."

"He has to be told immediately. His wife's condition is very serious. This has been a great shock for her."

One of Farfrae's men was sent to bring him back to Casterbridge.

Meanwhile, when the news of Lucetta's condition reached the street, the organizers of the skimmity-ride stopped it immediately and everyone disappeared into the night. The news also reached Henchard. He hurried to Farfrae's house to check on Lucetta. Elizabeth-Jane spoke to him at the front door and told him that her condition was not promising. Henchard went back to see how Lucetta was every hour that night. Although Lucetta calmed down a little when Farfrae returned, her condition didn't improve.

Henchard made his last visit at four o'clock in the morning. A servant was taking the cover off the doorbell outside, put there to stop people from ringing the bell and disturbing Lucetta.

"Why are you removing the cover?" asked Henchard.

"Because sir," replied the servant, "they can ring the bell as loud as they like now, she won't hear it anymore."

Henchard turned sadly toward home again. He and Farfrae had fought to have Lucetta, but in the end it was Death who got her.

Chapter 19

The return of the traveler

Henchard had not been home long when there was a knock on the door. It was Elizabeth-Jane.

"Have you heard about Mrs. Farfrae, Father?" she asked.

"Yes, I came from the house just a short while ago," he replied. "It's very good of you to come, Elizabeth-Jane. You must be exhausted, sitting up all night with her. You should stay here now till morning. Go and lie down in the other room and I'll call you when the breakfast is ready."

Elizabeth-Jane was not used to kind treatment like this from her father. Feeling both grateful and tired, she did as he said and lay down on the sofa in the next room. Henchard prepared the breakfast, but when it was ready he saw that Elizabeth-Jane had gone to sleep. He didn't disturb her, but waited patiently for her to wake up. The truth was that his feelings toward her had changed completely. Susan and Lucetta were gone and he had lost Farfrae as a friend long ago; he began to dream of sharing a future with this woman that was almost his daughter. However, his dream was interrupted by a knock on the door. He opened it and saw a large man with a kind, sun-tanned face.

"Good morning," said the stranger. "Is it Mr. Henchard?"

"Yes, it is."

"Could I have a few words with you?"

"Yes, of course," said Henchard, showing the way in.

"You may remember me?" said the stranger.

Henchard looked at him without much interest and shook his head.

"Or perhaps you don't. My name is Newson."

The light in Henchard's eyes seemed to die. "I know the name well," he said, staring at the floor.

"I don't doubt it," said Newson. "I've been looking for you for these past two weeks. I have come to talk about what happened over twenty years ago. It was a curious business."

"A curious business! I'm not the man you saw twenty years ago. I was not in my senses."

"We were both young and foolish," said Newson. "However, I've come to mend matters, not start arguments. I'd better tell you the part of the story that you don't know."

"Yes, please do," said Henchard. "Susan heard that you had died when your ship sank off Newfoundland."

"That was partly true – the ship did sink and most of the men did die. I survived because I managed to swim to the shore. When I thought about what to do next, I realized I had an opportunity to put right something that had been wrong for years. You see, Susan was not happy with me. She was certain she'd done the wrong thing in coming with me. Our relationship had no meaning for her. So I decided that if I let her think that I had in fact drowned, I would be giving her her freedom. She would go back to you and Elizabeth-Jane would have a home. This is the first time I've been back to England and I heard that she did go back to you, just as I thought. They told me that Susan was dead. But my Elizabeth-Jane – where is she?"

"Dead as well," said Henchard without a second thought. "Surely they told you that, too?"

"Dead!" said poor Newson, a look of pain coming over his face. "Where is she buried?"

"Beside her mother," replied Henchard, still staring at the floor.

"When did she die?"

"More than a year ago." Henchard was surprised at how easily the lies flew out of his mouth.

"Then my journey has been for nothing. It serves me right. I won't bother you anymore and I'll go back the way I came."

Henchard heard the sounds of Newson leaving the house and slowly walking away up the street. It was the walk of a sad man, thinking about his loss. A minute later he was gone. He had not even turned around to look back. He had simply believed Henchard's story and had not thought to ask him more questions, or check the truth of what he had heard. But would he be back? Henchard worried that Newson might return at anytime. But if he did, wasn't Elizabeth-Jane as much his daughter as Newson's? What was Newson's need compared to his? Newson's love for Elizabeth-Jane must have cooled down over the many years of their separation; whereas he, Henchard, felt that he had always been with her. And reasoning in this way, he believed his right to Elizabeth-Jane was greater than her father's.

Over the next few days he treated Elizabeth-Jane with a gentle kindness she had never seen in him. The knowledge that, at anytime, she might be taken away from him made his feelings for her stronger.

Elizabeth-Jane was lonely with Lucetta gone, and Henchard's caring attitude both surprised her and touched her heart.

They decided that she should move into the house with him. Under her gentle influence, he agreed to accept help from Farfrae and the town council. Thanks to them, Henchard and Elizabeth-Jane became the owners of a small seed and root store. Henchard alone would not have accepted this help, especially since it involved his old enemy Farfrae. However, for Elizabeth-Jane he was prepared to swallow his pride in a way that was entirely new to his character. The business did well and they were both grateful for each other's company.

The only shadow was Henchard's belief that Newson would certainly return at some time in the future. He lived in constant fear of hearing his knock on the door, and of Elizabeth-Jane learning that he had lied to her father and hidden the truth from her.

The weeks passed. The rest of the year went by peacefully and happily for Henchard and Elizabeth-Jane. Their root and seed business grew and they began to live more comfortably than before. Little by little the fear of Newson's return disappeared from Henchard's thoughts. Meanwhile, Farfrae was slowly getting over the loss of Lucetta. Another man might never have recovered, but Farfrae was too practical to think like this. Lucetta had told him everything about her past relationship with Henchard before her death. With the clear thinking that was part of his nature, he recognized that this would have made a happy marriage very difficult for them. In time, his deep sadness began to pass; he returned to work and filled the emptiness in his life with his day-to-day business.

It was perhaps only a matter of time before Farfrae's thoughts turned once again to the woman he had begun to love before Lucetta won his attention: Elizabeth-Jane. It started when they met walking outside Casterbridge. Farfrae then began to lend her books because, since the time that she lived with Lucetta, Elizabeth-Jane had read a great deal, in hopes of improving herself. Meeting each other when they could, often in the countryside outside Casterbridge so as not to be seen by curious eyes, their love grew little by little.

Henchard, however, was no fool. He began to notice that on certain occasions Elizabeth-Jane came home with little presents. He suspected that she and Farfrae were seeing each other. However, he was not the lion he once was and he did not ask her about it directly. He preferred to follow her on one of her walks and see what was happening with his own eyes. In this way he learned that they loved each other and planned to get married.

If she had given her heart to any other man, Henchard would have been glad. However, Farfrae was still his old enemy and he wondered if there was a way to scare him away from Elizabeth-Jane.

"Would he like her so much," he thought, "if he knew that she's not my daughter and that, in the eyes of the law, she's nobody's child? That would make him run off and then she'd stay with me."

Sometimes unwanted thoughts pop into our head, before we recognize them and send them back to where they came from.

"God help me!" he shouted out. "Why do I still have these evil thoughts, when I try so hard to keep them away?"

He never talked about Farfrae with Elizabeth-Jane, and she never mentioned anything to him either. He knew that after the last time, they would be unwilling to discuss their marriage with him, and that they would probably be very happy if he was out of the way. He wished he could escape from those that didn't want him and hide his head forever. This feeling grew stronger and stronger inside him and his health began to suffer.

One morning he was out walking in the countryside. In the distance he saw a man approaching Casterbridge on the Budmouth road. He expected it to be Farfrae, who sometimes came out here to meet Elizabeth-Jane on one of her walks. But as the man came closer, he saw that it was not Farfrae, but Newson.

Chapter 20

Leaving Casterbridge

The sailor stopped and seemed to be waiting for someone. Henchard knew immediately that Newson had come for his daughter. He had very little time left, so he immediately went home. There, he found Elizabeth-Jane.

"Oh, Father," she said, "I've had a strange letter, not signed. Somebody asked me to meet him either at noon on the Budmouth road or in the evening at Farfrae's. I don't understand it – should I go? I wanted to ask you first."

"Yes, go." Replied Henchard heavily. "I am going to leave Casterbridge, Elizabeth-Jane."

"Leave Casterbridge?" she cried. "And leave … me?"

"Yes, you can manage the shop²⁷ by yourself … and it's better if I go."

The tears ran silently down Elizabeth-Jane's face. She guessed that this decision of his must be because of Farfrae.

"I'm sorry you have decided to do this," she said. "I thought that Mr. Farfrae and I might get married in the future. I didn't know that you were against this idea."

"I agree with anything that you decide to do, my dear," he replied. "And if I didn't, it wouldn't matter. It's best that I go."

"But then you won't be able to come to my wedding and that's not right," she said.

"I can't … I can't. But think of me in your future life and don't let my mistakes, when you know them all, make you forget this – although my love for you came late, when it came it was strong. Please promise you won't forget me."

Nothing she could say could make him change his mind. He packed up his things and left, carrying what little he owned over his shoulder. He looked very similar to the man who had walked into Casterbridge twenty-five years ago, except this time his back was less straight, his step not as firm, and he was without the certainty and hope of youth.

* * *

A little while later, Elizabeth-Jane learned who the writer of that unsigned letter was, and Newson saw his daughter again for the first time in many years. He could not put into words the pride he felt on seeing the woman she had grown into, and he kissed her over and over again. It was a happy afternoon, spoiled only by the knowledge that Henchard had lied to them and so had delayed this joyful meeting for ten whole months. Newson, a gentle man that was not easily angered, didn't think badly of Henchard for what he had done, but his daughter was angry and wanted to forget Henchard completely.

Henchard walked for three days to see her on her wedding day, hoping that she would forgive him. However, when he arrived at the house, they were having the wedding reception and he was ashamed to go and speak to her in front of so many well-dressed guests. He asked a servant to tell the new Mrs. Farfrae that a simple friend wished to speak to her, and he waited for her in the kitchen. Elizabeth-Jane was shocked to find Henchard waiting to speak to her.

"Oh … it is you, Mr. Henchard," she said.

"What … you call me *Mr. Henchard*? I beg you, don't be so cold. You know everything now and your real father has taken my place, but please save a little room for me!"

"I could have loved you always," she cried, "I would have loved you gladly. But how can I, now that I know you lied to my father and me so cruelly?"

Henchard's mouth opened to start an explanation, to say he was sorry … but nothing came out. There were many things he could have said, but he didn't value himself enough to defend himself.

"I made a mistake in coming here today … I see that now. But it is only this once, so forgive me. I'll never trouble you again, Elizabeth-Jane, not till my dying day. Good-bye!"

Then, before she could collect her thoughts, he went out of the room and out of the house through the back way.

∗   ∗   ∗

After the wedding, the excitement of recent events slowly died down. Newson stayed at Farfrae's house for three more days before deciding that he needed to live in a place where he could see the sea. So he moved to Budmouth and bought a little house there that had a view of the sea. Farfrae continued to do well in business and his life carried on much like before, though now he hurried home more quickly after business hours.

Elizabeth-Jane took on the job of managing the house. During her work, she had plenty of time to think about the last time she had seen Henchard and slowly her anger left her. She realized that he had come to her wedding in order to ask for her forgiveness and she decided she wanted to see him again. She and Farfrae agreed that they would try and find Henchard and have him live somewhere nearby so that she could take care of him.

After a few days of searching, they found the house where Henchard was supposed to be living. Elizabeth-Jane prepared the words she would say to Henchard in her mind. As they walked toward the house, a farm worker came out.

"Excuse me, is this where Mr. Henchard lives?" asked Elizabeth-Jane.

"Are you relatives?" asked the farm worker.

"No … well, in fact yes," replied Elizabeth-Jane. "Is he here?"

"No, Madam, I'm afraid he's gone now."

"Gone? What do you mean, gone?" asked Elizabeth-Jane, her voice shaking.

"I'm afraid he wasn't well, Madam," answered the farm

worker. "You see, he came here about a week ago and asked if he could rent a room. He wouldn't eat anything at all. He had no appetite. He just got weaker and weaker and today he died, just four hours ago."

"How terrible!" said Farfrae. "It doesn't seem possible."

Elizabeth-Jane started crying.

"He left a note on his bed. Look, here it is."

They read the note:

106

The last wishes of Michael Henchard:
Elizabeth-Jane should not be told of my death.
I do not wish to be buried in holy ground.
No bells should be rung for me.
No one should come and see my dead body.
No one should come to my funeral.
No flowers should be planted on my grave.
No man is to remember me.
I sign this document:

Michael Henchard

"What bitterness in these lines!" said Elizabeth-Jane through her tears. "If only I hadn't been so unkind to him the last time we met. But that can never be changed now."

Nevertheless, she knew that the man who wrote these words meant them and, as much as possible, she respected his wishes.

* * *

For many weeks she felt deep pain because he had suffered so much and because she had misunderstood him on her wedding day. But, as time passed, this slowly disappeared. Her life with Farfrae was a peaceful, happy one. In quiet moments she was often surprised that so much happiness had come to her in adult life, when, as a young woman, she had felt that happiness was nothing more than a few brief moments in a general drama of pain. She learned that life always brought the unexpected, and that happiness was to be found by taking pleasure in the small satisfactions that life offered and by helping those around her do the same.

LOOKING BACK

. . . .

1 Check your answer to *Looking forward* on page 87.

ACTIVITIES

. . . .

2 Match the two parts of the sentences.
1 Lucetta is worried that Henchard ☐
2 When Farfrae listens to Henchard reading the letters, he ☐
3 In the end, Henchard doesn't tell people about the letters because he ☐
4 When Jopp is in Peter's Finger, he ☐
5 When Lucetta sees the people on her street, she ☐

a doesn't want to hurt Lucetta.
b will use their love letters to hurt her.
c shows Lucetta's letters to everyone.
d realizes that everyone knows about her relationship with Henchard.
e doesn't know that Lucetta wrote them.

3 Put the sentences about Newson's life in order.
1 His ship sinks. ☐
2 Henchard tells him that Elizabeth-Jane is dead. ☐
3 He writes a letter to Elizabeth-Jane. ☐
4 He buys a house in Budmouth. ☐
5 He stays in Casterbridge for a few days, after his daughter's wedding. ☐
6 He comes back to live in England. ☐
7 He decides to let Susan think he is dead. ☐

4 Read the sentences from the text and answer the questions.

1 It was only a question of time before Farfrae heard about these threats. (page 88)
What are the threats?

2 "You know what's needed here? A skimmity-ride." (page 93)
What is this? What reasons are given for doing it?

3 "... they can ring the bell as loud as they like now, she won't hear it anymore." (page 97)
What has happened?

4 "Oh ... it is you, Mr. Henchard ..." (page 104)
Why does Elizabeth-Jane talk to Henchard like this?

5 ... she was often surprised that so much happiness had come to her in adult life ... (page 107)
What makes Elizabeth-Jane happy at the end of the story? Why does it surprise her?

5 Answer the questions.

1 How do Jopp's actions help cause Lucetta's death?

2 How do Henchard's feelings for Elizabeth-Jane change after Lucetta dies?

3 Why didn't Newson tell Susan that he was alive after his ship sank?

Glossary

[1]**furmity** (page 6) *noun*   a dish made of **wheat** that is boiled in milk and sweetened with fruit or other ingredients

[2]**corn** (page 6) *noun*   the seeds of plants such as **wheat**, oats, maize or barley, or the plant itself

[3]**shilling** (page 7) *noun*   a unit of money worth five pence and used in Britain until 1971

[4]**auctioneer** (page 9) *noun*   the person that calls out the prices at an auction, or public sale of goods to the person that offers the highest price

[5]**guinea** (page 9) *noun*   an old British coin worth one pound and one **shilling**

[6]**wheat** (page 19) *noun*   a plant with yellow-brown grain used for making flour for bread, or the grain itself

[7]**harvest** (page 19) *noun*   the time of year when crops like **wheat** are cut and collected from the fields

[8]**hay** (page 27) *noun*   grass which is cut and dried and used as animal food

[9]**coach** (page 27) *noun*   and old-fashioned vehicle pulled by one or more horses

[10]**fate** (page 29) *noun*   a power that some people believe controls all events, so that you cannot control or change the way things will happen

[11]**sovereign** (page 34) *noun*   an old British coin worth one pound and used in Britain from 1817 to 1914

[12]**seal** (page 34) *verb*   to close something (e.g. a letter)

[13]**make up for** (page 40)   to compensate for something bad with something good

[14]**ill** (page 40) *adjective*   British English for 'sick'

[15]**scandal** (page 40) *noun*   (an action or an event that causes) a public feeling of shock or strong moral disapproval

[16]**deal** (page 44) *noun*   an agreement or an arrangement, especially in business

[17]**deserve** (page 45) *verb*   to have earned something or be given something because of your actions or qualities

[18]**carriage** (page 58) *noun*   a vehicle with four wheels, which is usually pulled by horses and was used especially in the past

[19]**frustrated** (page 60) *adjective*   when you feel annoyed or discouraged because you cannot achieve what you want

[20]**debt** (page 70) *noun*   something owed, especially money

[21]**profit** (page 74) *noun*   money that is earned in trade or business, especially after paying the costs of producing and selling goods or services

[22]**courtroom** (page 78) *noun*   a room where a court of law meets to decide on trials or other legal cases

[23]**rum** (page 78) *noun*   a strong alcoholic drink made from the juice of the sugar cane plant

[24]**conscience** (page 80) *noun*   the part of you that judges the morality of your own actions and makes you feel guilty about bad things you have done

[25]**councilor** (page 88) *noun*   an elected member of a local government

[26]**skimmity-ride** (page 93) *noun*   a way of showing public disapproval in the past, where models of a man and a woman were placed on a horse and ridden around the town and made fun of

[27]**shop** (page 103) *noun*   British English for 'store'